NORTH NECHES RIVER NATIONAL WILDLIFE REFUGE ESTABLISHMENT PROPOSAL, ENVIRONMENTAL ASSESSMENT, CONCEPTUAL MANAGEMENT PLAN, & LAND PROTECTION PLAN

United States Fish and Wildlife Service
National Wildlife Refuge System
Southwest Region, Albuquerque, New Mexico
March 2005

1

Table of Contents

I. PURPOSE AND NEED FOR ACTION

Proposed Action Project Overview – Establishment of an Acquisition Boundary

The U.S. Fish and Wildlife Service (Service) proposes to establish a new National Wildlife Refuge in East Texas along a 38 mile reach of the upper portion of the Neches River dividing Anderson and Cherokee Counties. (See Appendix 2). According to the

 Preliminary Project Proposal approved in 1988, the refuge would be approximately 35 miles south-southeast of Tyler and 100 miles southeast of Dallas. The proposed refuge is located on both sides of the Neches River and includes overflow bottomlands and adjacent pine and pine/hardwood forests.

If approved, the establishment of the refuge will then allow the Service to initiate proposals for the acquisition of lands within an acquisition boundary, up to 25,281 acres, within that boundary. The scope and dimensions of the proposed boundary and an alternative are the subjects of this environmental assessment (EA). A refuge will only exist after an interest in land is acquired by the United States and therefore included into the National Wildlife Refuge System (NWRS). Establishment of the refuge acquisition boundary would allow the Service to acquire from willing sellers lands within that boundary.

The Service will manage acquired lands in order to conserve, protect and enhance a diversity of habitats and the wildlife resources thereon. Such management will be in accord with the authorities granted to the Service under the National Wildlife Refuge System Improvement Act of 1997 and other statutes governing the management of fish and wildlife resources on NWRS lands. Other authorities affecting the acquisition of interest in land and the management of those lands are listed in Appendix A.

Refuge Purposes – Should the Service establish the Neches River National Wildlife Refuge, the purposes of the refuge would be to: (1) protect nesting, wintering and migratory habitat for migratory birds of the Central Flyway; (2) protect the bottomland hardwood forests for their diverse biological values and wetland functions of water quality improvement and flood control assistance; and, (3) provide for compatible wildlife-dependent recreation opportunities in accordance with the National Wildlife Refuge System Improvement Act of 1997. The actual refuge purposes would be cited specifically as:

- ... For use as an inviolate sanctuary, or for any other management purpose, for migratory birds. 16 U.S.C. sec. 715d (Migratory Bird Conservation Act)

- ... the conservation of the wetlands of the Nation in order to maintain the public benefits they provide and to help fulfill international obligations contained in various migratory bird treaties and conventions ... 16 U.S.C. sec 3901(b), 100 Stat. 3583 (Emergency Wetlands Resources Act of 1986)
- "...for the development, advancement, management, conservation, and protection of fish and wildlife resources ..." 16 U.S.C. sec. 742f(a)(4) "... for the benefit of the United States Fish and Wildlife Service, in performing its activities and services. Such acceptance may be subject to the terms of any restrictive or affirmative covenant, or condition of servitude ..." 16 U.S.C. sec. 742f(b)(1) (Fish and Wildlife Act of 1956)

Need for Federal Action of Establishment of a Refuge

Over the past two decades, the Service has been committed to protecting habitats in all regions of the United States. These habitats include the dwindling bottomland-hardwood resources in riparian and wetland areas that are home to a number of species of migratory birds, mammals, riparian and others dependent on these forested areas. The Neches River has most recently been identified by the Texas Parks and Wildlife Department, the Conservation Fund and other entities as an area, of extreme importance to the diversity of wildlife in east Texas, which is being affected by the expansion of urban populations and other types of development.

Texas Bottomland Hardwood Concept Plan and the Preliminary Project Proposal

In 1985, the Fish and Wildlife Service identified this reach of the Neches River as important in its Texas Bottomland Hardwood Concept Plan and in its Land Protection Plan for Bottomland Hardwoods, Category 3, Texas and Oklahoma. The Service listed the "Neches River North" as a Priority 1 protection need.

In 1988, the Service Directorate approved the Preliminary Project Proposal to proceed in the development of more detailed planning for a 25,281 acre refuge in the upper Neches area. At that time, land costs were estimated at approximately $18 million. Those costs today would be nearly $33 million. The approval letter dated January 6, 1988, stated that the "waterfowl use numbers, when determined during the detailed planning phase, should determine whether Migratory Bird Conservation Funds, Land and Water Conservation Funds, or a combination of both shall be the funding source for this unit." The proposal states:

> "The Neches River National Wildlife Refuge is being proposed to preserve bottom-land hardwoods that are important wintering habitat for mallards and wood ducks and production habitat for wood ducks. This proposal is designed to assist in meeting the habitat goals presented in the Ten-Year Waterfowl Habitat Acquisition Report (Category 3) and the North American Waterfowl Management Plan. The proposed area also protects a large number of other wildlife and plant species and will be of potential benefit to the federally endangered bald eagle and red-

cockaded woodpecker, the threatened American Alligator, and several State species of special concern."

Real Estate acquisition components common to Alternatives

- Willing Sellers Only -- Although the Service, like all agencies of the United States Government, has condemnation authority, it is the Service's policy to acquire land and interests in land from <u>willing sellers only</u>. No lands have been condemned in the past for any refuge in Texas, and the Service does not propose condemnation of any lands in the future. The Service can acquire land or interests in land <u>only</u> within an approved refuge boundary. In fact, the Service can't even accept a donation of land outside of an approved refuge boundary. Lands in any of the refuge boundary expansions would be acquired only from willing sellers as funding becomes available. Landowners within an expanded refuge boundary would be completely free to keep their land, to sell their land to whoever they wished, to leave their land to their heirs, or to change uses of their land. Including lands within a NWR boundary does not require the landowner to sell only to the Service nor does it limit that landowner's other conservation options and opportunities. The Service actively encourages all private landowners who are interested in wildlife or environmental conservation, whether their lands are within an approved refuge boundary or not, to avail themselves of the many conservation programs and options available.

    Since 1971, the acquisition of land for a variety of Federal government programs and projects has been subject to the Uniform Relocation and Assistance and Real Property Acquisition Policies Act of 1970, as amended in 1987 (the Uniform Act). The full rules for the Uniform Act can be found in the Code of Federal Regulations, Title 49, Part 24. The Uniform Act applies to the Service's land acquisition program and two very important provisions of this Act affect willing sellers: 1) relocation assistance for sellers of land, and 2) the requirement to offer to purchase for the full fair market value as established by an approved appraisal. The relocation provisions provide financial assistance to landowners, tenants, and small business owners who are required to move because of the sale of real property, in whole or part, to the Service. The relocation assistance is provided so that displaced persons will not suffer disproportionate injuries as a result of programs designed for the benefit of the public as a whole. Fair market value appraisals are done to ensure that potential sellers will be treated fairly, consistently, and equitably. The appraisal is independent, impartial, prepared by a qualified appraiser, and reviewed to ensure that all applicable appraisal standards and requirements were met. The amount the Service offers to purchase the land will never be less than the fair market value established by the approved appraisal. The Service also pays all of the incidental expenses incurred in transferring title; such as recording fees, title insurance costs, necessary surveys, escrow fees, and other similar expenses.

- Acquisition methods -- For all land and interests in land acquired by the Service, title is taken by the United States of America. The Service acquires most land in one of two ways: 1) in fee, or 2) conservation easement. The "fee" means virtually all of the rights and interests in the land, that which would be generally recognized as "ownership of the land". Fee acquisition removes the land from the tax rolls. Fee acquisition gives the

Service exclusive possession and use of the land which would allow for compatible public recreational activities. Fee acquisition allows the Service to perform any of the management activities (i.e. water control, burning, etc.) deemed necessary for habitat conservation on that land. The fee acquisitions are typically subject to reserved or outstanding subsurface mineral interests and other existing surface easements, such as pipelines or other rights-of-way.

- The purchase of a conservation easement is the acquisition of a much lesser interest in the land. "Ownership of the land" does not transfer to the United States and the land remains on the tax rolls with the underlying private landowner having the tax obligations. Conservation easements can consist of one or both of the following categories of interests in land: 1) negative covenants, which prevent a specific use (i.e. no development) and 2) possessory interests, which grant a specific use right (i.e. public hunting). Conservation easements are an acquisition option when adequate habitat conservation can be achieved without the Service acquiring full ownership of the land. Conservation easements are not always a viable option with willing sellers because some sellers wish to dispose of all of their interests in the land for various reasons. Conservation easements are appraised and purchased in the same way as fee acquisitions. Also, the Service generally accepts donations of both fee and conservation easements.

The Service will consider both fee and conservation easement for future acquisitions dependent upon the habitat conservation requirements and the willing seller's agreement.

In a few instances, the Service acquires interests in land by lease, right-of-way easement, or agreement. These are typically either for a shorter period of time or for more limited use purposes compared to fee and conservation easements.

- Acquisition funding sources -- The Service has only two primary land acquisition funding sources: 1) the Migratory Bird Conservation Fund, and 2) the Land and Water Conservation Fund. The Migratory Bird Hunting and Conservation Stamp Act of 1934, as amended (16 U.S.C. 718-718h) requires all waterfowl hunters 16 years of age and over to annually purchase and carry a Federal Duck Stamp. Approximately 98 cents of every Duck Stamp dollar goes directly into the Migratory Bird Conservation Fund to purchase wetlands and wildlife habitat for inclusion into the National Wildlife Refuge System. Since 1934, more than $500 million has gone into this Fund to purchase more than 5 million acres of primarily waterfowl habitat. The Fund is administered by the Migratory Bird Conservation Commission and acquisition expenditures from this Fund require the approval of the governor of the state where the land to be purchased is located.

The other primary land acquisition funding source was authorized by the Land and Water Conservation Fund Act of 1965, as amended (16 U.S.C. 4601-11). The Land and Water Conservation Fund (LWCF) appropriations are derived from outer continental shelf oil & gas leases, tax on motorboat fuels, and the sale of certain surplus Federal lands. Forty per cent or more of LWCF are appropriated for Federal land acquisition for the National Park System, the National Forest System, the National Wildlife Refuge System, and the Bureau of Land Management. The balance of the Funds provides financial assistance to the States for planning, land acquisition, and development of outdoor recreation opportunities. The LWCF is not a discretionary funding source and Congress appropriates money to a specific project or refuge for land acquisition.

- Refuge Revenue Sharing -- Lands acquired by the Service in fee are removed from the tax rolls, because as an agency of the United States Government, the Service, like city, township, county and state governments, is exempt from taxation. Those lands in which the Service only acquires a conservation easement remain on the tax rolls and the tax obligation remains with the private landowner. The Refuge Revenue Sharing Act (the Act of June 15, 1935, as amended in 1978 by Public Law 95-469) or (16 U.S.C. 715s) authorizes the Service to make payments to the county or other local unit of government to offset the tax losses for lands administered solely or primarily by the Service. The net income the Service receives from the sale of products or privileges on refuges (like timber sales, grazing fees, right-of-way permit fees, etc.) is deposited in the National Wildlife Refuge Fund for revenue sharing payments. Originally, 25% of the net receipts collected from the sale of various products or privileges from refuge lands were paid to the counties in which they were located. However, if no revenue was generated from the refuge lands, the county received no payment. The Refuge Revenue Sharing Act was amended in 1964 to allow a payment of either (1) 25% of the net receipts, (2) ¾ of 1% of the adjusted purchase price of refuge land, or (3) 75 cents per acre, whichever was greater, on acquired lands. Payments still had to be made out of refuge receipts in the National Wildlife Refuge Fund. Beginning in Fiscal Year 1976, the refuge receipts were not sufficient to make the county payments and the payments were reduced accordingly. Partly because of this, the Refuge Revenue Sharing Act was again amended in 1978. This amendment allowed Congress to appropriate funds to make up any shortfall in the revenue sharing fund. It also approved use of the payments for any governmental purpose; whereas, before, the payments could only be used for roads and schools.

Because refuge receipts have not kept up with the general increase in property values, the ¾ of 1% of market value of refuge lands has effectively become the largest amount of refuge revenue sharing payment allowable under the Act since 1976. Initially, Congress appropriated the additional funds necessary to make the largest payment, but only through Fiscal Year 1980. Since that time Congress has not appropriated sufficient additional funds to make the largest payment allowed by law. If the amount Congress appropriates is not enough to match the largest payment allowable, the units of local government receive a pro-rata share. Even without the full supplemental appropriations, the dollar amount of Refuge Revenue Sharing payments is substantial and significantly offsets the local tax losses. In some instances, largely for lands subject to the agricultural exemption, the Refuge Revenue Sharing payments have been equal to or even greater than the amount paid in taxes while in private ownership. The Service supports full Congressional appropriations to achieve the maximum Refuge Revenue Sharing payments.

The Refuge Revenue Sharing payments are usually made during the first quarter of each calendar year. By law the Service makes the payments to the unit of local government that levies and collects general purpose real property taxes, which in Texas, is the county government.

II. ALTERNATIVES

Alternative A- No Action (Non- Establishment of Refuge)

Under this alternative, the Service would not establish the Neches River National Wildlife Refuge. Individual landowners could still have the option to pursue land conservation measures on their own, including applying for state or federal grants or cost-sharing habitat improvement projects.

The current trend among the nation's large timber companies is to divest themselves from many of their large land holdings. Land investment and development-oriented companies, sometimes including large insurance or retirement fund investment companies, mark the current market for these divestitures. Two of the three larger land ownerships in the project area have already been on the market. Nationwide, large landholdings tend to be subdivided over time, with subsequent sales, because land markets favor increased subdivision. Although the floodplain status of much of the Neches River bottomland within the study area discourages building there, building could occur on the upland areas. Another trend, in the uplands study area, is forest clearing for pastures, tree farms, and residences. Leasing of land for hunting would likely continue on many forested tracts. Market incentives for logging could be increased in future years depending on what occurs in the world timber market. Increased demand for lumber products will likely be accelerated as world population growth continues.

Alternative B- Establish Acquisition Boundary to include up to 25,281 Acres

Under this alternative, the Service would establish the Neches River National Wildlife Refuge using the acquisition boundary shown on the Overview Map in Appendix II. This alternative encompasses 25,281 acres and includes lands outside the main riparian area that are considered drainage to the Neches. Also included are pine forest upland areas that would enhance the diversity of wildlife and prevent encroachment to the riparian zone. The river reach encompassed by this alternative spans approximately 38 miles. It also includes part of the watershed of Wells (a.k.a Hurricane) Creek noted for its high quality forest habitat.

Alternative C – Establish Acquisition Boundary to include up to 15,294 Acres

Under this alternative, the Service would establish the Neches River National Wildlife Refuge using the acquisition boundary shown on the Overview Map in Appendix II. The configuration of this boundary encompasses 15,294 acres and is based upon a priority of acquiring lands considered riparian wetlands along with associated bottomland hardwood habitat. This alternative would eliminate acquisition of associated pine forests or areas not directly in a narrower riparian corridor. Lands could be acquired by conservation easement or in fee title, depending on the sellers' preferences. It would take a number of years for the Refuge to be fully acquired because it depends on the presence of willing sellers and the availability of funding. While this alternative also includes the large landholdings of Alternative B, it is more environmentally selective in that its acquisition priorities would focus solely on drainage and river bottoms and where possible exclude upland and pine plantation properties.

Acquisition Estimated Cost

The current total estimated acquisition cost of a refuge containing 25,281 acres is approximately $33 million and is based on recent comparable sales. The eventual cost may fluctuate depending on the market trends in area real estate markets. The estimated acquisition cost of a refuge containing 15,294 acres is approximately $20 million.

III. AFFECTED ENVIRONMENT

Climate and Air Quality

The project area is characterized by a modified marine or subtropical climate (Larkin and Bomar 1983). The primary influence on this climatic type is the onshore flow of tropical air from the Gulf of Mexico. Annual rainfall averages between 43 and 46 inches for the two counties (Dallas Morning News 2004). Summers can be hot and humid, while winters can be mild with some frosts between late November and early March.

Air quality is generally good in the two counties because the area is still primarily rural and does not have much heavy industry or population compared to urban counties.

Geology and Soils

The project area lies within the Gulf Coastal Plain Physiographic Province (Johnson 1931). The elevation on the site varies from approximately 265 feet above mean sea level, along the Neches River along the central portion of the site to nearly 600 feet on White Mountain in the east central portion of the site. The project area is drained by Worley Branch, Oak Creek, Walnut Branch, Wells (a.k.a. Hurricane) Creek, Beech Creek, Tailes Creek and ultimately by the Neches River, which flows through the center of the area. The geological substrate of the project site is formed by five different groups: (1) the surficial, recent alluvium (Quaternary System and Holocene Series), (2) the fluviatile terrace deposit (Quaternary System and Pleistocene Series), (3) the Sparta Sand Formation (Tertiary System and Eocene Series), (4) the Weches Formation (Tertiary System and Eocene Series) and (5) the Queen City Sand Formation (Tertiary System and Eocene Series) (Renfro et al. 1973, Shelby et al. 1968).

The recent alluvial materials of the Neches River and major tributary creeks are primarily made up of the following types of soils: clays, silts, sands and some organic materials (Formed 40-60 million years ago): These have been classified as follows: the Sparta Sands, Weches Formation, and Queen City Sands (from youngest to oldest, respectively). The Sparta Sands and Weches Formation outcrops are located along the northeastern and east central boundary. Sparta Sands are composed of fine-grained quartz particles mixed with some lignitic clay and silt particles, and may be over 200 feet in thickness. The Weches deposits, varying in thickness for 50-90 feet, are composed of Glauconite, quartz sand, and clay with numerous marine fossils. The Queen City Sands, approaching 325 feet in thickness, border the alluvial and fluviatile deposits to the east and west. These deposits are primarily fine-grained quartz sands interbedded with clay.

Five soil series, correlated with the geological formations, are found on the project site: (1) The Nahatche series with in the floodplains, (2) The Bienville series form on the floodplain terraces, (3) the Cuthbert series on the uplands adjacent to the floodplain, (4) the Trawick series found on the higher elevations associated with the Weches Formation, and (5) Lilbert series found on the highest elevations associated with the Sparta Sands (Mowery 1959, Coffee 1975, and Raymond Dolezel, Soil Conservation Service, Nacogdoches personal communications).

- The Nahatche soils are deep, nearly level loams on the floodplains of the Neches River and its larger tributaries. These soils are somewhat poorly drained and slightly acidic although less acidic than most bottomland soils.

-

- The Bienville soils are deep and somewhat excessively drained sands (water located at 4-8 feet below the surface) on river terraces. These soils are slightly to moderately acidic.

-

- The Cuthbert series consists of moderately deep, well drained loamy or sandy loam soils associated with the Queen City Sands geological formation. The soils are slightly to strongly acidic.

-

- The Trawick series consists of deep, well-drained loamy soils on uplands. These soils are formed in glauconitic green/sand marls of the Weches Formation, and the soils range from moderate to very strongly acidic.

-

- The Lilbert soils consist of deep, well-drained sands on uplands of the Sparta Sand formation. The soils are slightly to very strongly acidic.

Water Resources

The Neches River is one of the largest rivers in east Texas. It originates in Van Zandt County, flows approximately 280 miles to its confluence with the Angelina River and empties into the Gulf of Mexico in Orange County near Port Neches for a total reach of roughly 420 miles. At the north end of the project area the river has flows from a maximum peak of 26,900 cfs to a slowest daily mean of 3.3 cfs. Lake Palestine, upstream from the project area is the only reservoir on the upper

reach of the River. B.A. Steinhagen Reservoir (also known as Town Bluff Reservoir or Dam B Reservoir) is located downstream in Tyler and Jasper Counties at the confluence with the Angelina River.

The project area is drained by Worley Branch, Oak Creek, Walnut Branch, Wells (a.k.a. Hurricane) Creek, Beech Creek, Tailes Creek and ultimately by the Neches River, which flows through the center of the site.

In 2002 the Texas Parks and Wildlife Department nominated the Neches River segment between the Hopson Mill Creek confluence in Jasper/Tyler Counties upstream to the Blackburn Crossing in

14

Anderson/Cherokee Counties as an "ecologically significant river segment (TNRCC stream segment 0604). This segment includes the proposed refuge study area. However, the Texas legislature has not confirmed this nomination.

The Texas Committee on Natural Resources, a non-governmental organization, has proposed that the Upper Neches River be designated as a National Scenic River between Lake Palestine and the B.A. Steinhagen Reservoir.

A reservoir on the Neches River was proposed in the 1980's within the project area as a result of a U. S. Army Corps of Engineers feasibility study. It was first called the Weches Reservoir proposal, but is now called the Fastrill Reservoir proposal. This proposal did not appear as a recommendation in the 2002 Water for Texas report by the Texas Water Development Board. While the project is still considered a long-term possibility, already the City of Dallas along with the Upper Neches Water Authority has contracted the development of a feasibility study regarding the development of a reservoir. The City of Dallas is aware of the refuge proposal and will develop the feasibility study keeping in mind the potential impact to a refuge designed to protect bottomland resources that would be eliminated by inundation by a reservoir.

A near term major reservoir proposal in Cherokee County is Lake Columbia (formerly Lake Eastex) located east of the project area. That reservoir proposal is undergoing the permitting process now. It would dam Mud Creek, not the Neches River.

There are some water quality problems affecting the Neches River from local oil drilling sites. Flooding of drilling pads, overflow pits, and tank batteries can be a problem during high water events. Runoff from highways and other non-point sources also contribute to decreased water quality. However, the River also filters out some pollutants as water passes through the numerous marshes, beaver dams, and forested wetlands on its main stem. A diversion structure within the project area near Rocky Point withdraws some of the River's flow to supply Palestine's municipal water needs.

Vegetation

The project area lies within the Pineywoods Vegetation Region and Oak-Hickory-Pine Forest sub region of Texas (Fish and Wildlife Service 1979). The project area is vegetated by bottomland hardwood forests and shrub swamps with minor amounts of aquatic beds, emergent

beds, open water and forested swamps in the floodplains. Upland areas outside of the floodplain are primarily pine plantations (recently planted to nearing maturity) and mixed pine-hardwood forests.

Plant Communities The bottomlands are primarily classified as temporarily inundated, broad and narrow-leaf deciduous forests (Cowardin et al. 1979). The black willow *(Salix nigra)* forest type occurs as a pioneer community type on the point bars and low levees of the Neches River. The major portion of the bottomlands can be classified as a willow oak *(Quercus phellos)*, water oak *(Q. nigra)* and sweet gum *(Liquidambar styraciflua)* type found on the ridges and higher flats. The lower flats and back swamps are dominated by overcup oak *(Quercus lyrata)*, bitter pecan or water hickory *(Carya aquatica)* and water elm *(Planera aquatica)*. Other important over story species include black gum *(Nyssa sylvatica)*, southern red oak (Quercus falcata), swamp chestnut oak *(Quercus michauxii)*, and loblolly pine *(Pinus taeda)*.

The bottomland forest types have a diverse midstory and under story component. Common midstory species in the Neches River include yaupon *(Ilex vomitoria)*, possum haw *(I. decidua)*, American hornbeam *(Carpinus caroliniana)*, and red maple *(Acer rubrum)*. Important woody vines include poison ivy *(Rhus toxicodendron)*, greenbriers *(Smilax* spp.)*, rattan or supple jack *(Berchemia scandens)*, and grape *(Vitis* spp.)*. Important grasses in the bottomlands include giant cane *(Arundinaria gigantea)*, inland sea oats *(Chasmanthium latifolium)*, and wild rye *(Elymus* spp.)*.

The wettest sites along sloughs are dominated by shrub swamps composed of water elm, buttonbush *(Cephalanthus occidentalis)*, and western may haw *(Crataegus opaca)*. Shrub swamps are a major vegetation type within the project area. Forested swamps of cypress *(Taxodium distichum)* are very rare in the project area. Other wetland types within the floodplains include emergent aquatic beds, floating aquatic beds, and marshes on and adjacent to the numerous oxbows and sloughs such as Dead Water Lake, Buzzard Slough, Twin Lakes, Alligator Lake, Black Lake, Phillips Lake, and Indian Pond. These areas are dominated by smartweeds *(Persicaria* spp.)*, arrowheads *(Sagittaria* spp.)*, cattails *(Typha* spp.)*, water lilies (Nymphaea spp.), lotus *(Nelumbo lutea)*, spatterdock *(Nuphar advena)* and duckweed *(Lemna* spp.)*.

The upland portion of the project area is largely in pine plantations and mixed pine hardwood forests. The plantations are primarily loblolly pines *(Pinus taeda)* with minor amounts of the introduced slash pine *(Pinus elliottii)*.

It is not known if the federal candidate species Neches River rose mallow is found in the project area.

Two plant species of special concern have been documented in the Neches River project area, a shrub called the Texas spice tree and a tiny herbaceous plant known only by its scientific name *Geocarpum minimum.* Other species of potential occurrence include the wing seed sedge *(Carex alata),* a peripheral species listed by the Texas Natural Heritage Program, found in Anderson County in mud and wet, sandy, loam soils. The hawthorn *(Crataegus warneri),* an endemic species listed by the Texas Natural Heritage Program and a possible federal candidate, is also found in Anderson and Cherokee Counties in sandy woods and on dry banks (U.S. Fish and Wildlife Service 1987).

Fish and Wildlife

The diverse flora of the bottomland ecosystem, a result of numerous physical factors, supports an equally diverse fauna. Diversity of most animal groups is greater in bottomlands than in other adjacent upland habitat types because of the diversity of floral species and the abundance of food resources, including the bountiful crops of mast (fruit) of hardwood species.

Waterfowl

One of the many important values of bottomlands and associated wetlands is to waterfowl species. The primary emphasis of the proposed bottomland hardwood habitat protection program is the perpetuation of waterfowl species dependent on east Texas bottomlands (Fish and Wildlife Service 1985). In the process of preserving bottomland hardwood habitat for waterfowl, a large number of other wildlife species benefit. The bottomland hardwoods of eastern Texas contain important wintering habitat for various waterfowl species, including the mallard, as well as vital producing and rearing habitat for the wood duck. Historically, the area has played a key role in sustaining the Central Flyway waterfowl population. Eastern Texas and Oklahoma bottomland hardwoods represent the only significant breeding habitat of the wood duck and one of the most important wintering areas for the mallard in the Central Flyway.

The project area is reported to have the highest population of waterfowl in the Upper Neches River Basin. The Fish and Wildlife Service has acknowledged the importance of this area along with adjacent Oklahoma bottomlands and the Mississippi River Floodplain. The bottomland hardwoods of Arkansas, Louisiana, Oklahoma, Mississippi, Tennessee, Kentucky, Missouri, Illinois, Iowa, and Texas have been proposed by the Fish and Wildlife Service as Category 3 for habitat preservation based on its importance to waterfowl (Fish and Wildlife Service 1984 and 1985 supplement). The region is of primary importance to the mallard and wood duck.

The mallard has the most extensive breeding range of any duck in North America, extending from the shores of the Bering Sea through the northern one-third of the United States (Bellrose 1976). A significant number of mallards winter in the bottomlands of east Texas, but their number varies considerably from year to year

(Figure 5). Bellrose (1976) has estimated that over 120,000 birds utilize eastern Texas (approximately 15,000 on the Texas coast). Over 30 percent of the North American mallard population winters within waterfowl habitat category 3.

The wood duck regularly breeds from southern Canada to the Gulf of Mexico. The lower Mississippi River Delta and east Texas and Oklahoma are among the most important wood duck production areas. The interior migratory pattern extends throughout the south from the Carolinas to eastern Texas. Over 900,000 wood ducks of the interior population winter in Alabama, Mississippi, Arkansas, Louisiana, and Texas. Wood ducks consistently utilize natural wetlands for wintering and breeding habitat (Knauer 1977, Taylor 1977, Fredrickson 1980). Several wood duck roosts are present in the project area and a significant wood duck nesting population occurs in the area.

One of the primary migration corridors for dabbling ducks is through eastern Texas. This corridor is utilized by almost 3 million dabbling ducks (Bellrose 1968). The principal species migrating through and to the lesser extent, wintering in east Texas, besides mallards and wood ducks, include the green-winged teal *(Anas crecca)*, blue-winged teal *(Anas discors)*, northern pintail *(Anas acuta)*, northern shoveler *(Anas clypeata)*, Gadwall *(Anas strepera)*, and American widgeon *(Anas americana)*.

The area is of lesser importance as a migratory route and wintering waterfowl area for both diving ducks and geese. Over the years, waterfowl hunting has been a very important form of local recreation.

Other Birds

A total of 273 species of birds occur in the bottomland forests and associated wetlands in eastern Texas (Fish and Wildlife Service 1985). Included in this list are 38 waterfowl species; 29 colonial water birds (i.e., herons, gulls, and terns); 20 hawks, vultures and owls; 37 rails and shorebirds; 8 woodpeckers; 130 passerine birds; and 11 miscellaneous species. A total of 101 species are known or believed to breed in eastern Texas. The project site is of importance to a number of colonial water birds, raptors, woodpeckers, and passerine birds, particularly warblers, vireos, and flycatchers (Fish and Wildlife Service 1985).

Mammals

A total of 45 mammal species have been recorded in the bottomlands and associated wetlands of east Texas. Included are 11 species of bats, 15 species of rodents (including squirrels), 11 species of carnivores, and 8 miscellaneous species (Fish and Wildlife Service 1985). Important game species that occur on the project site include the swamp rabbit *(Sylvilagus aquaticus)*, gray squirrel *(Sciurus carolinensis)*, and white-tailed deer.

The principal furbearers that occur (or potentially occur) on the project area are the raccoon, opossum *(Didelphis virginiana)*, gray fox *(Urocyon cinereoargenteus)*, bobcat *(Felis rufus)*, Coyote *(Canis latrans)*, striped skunk *(Mephitis mephitis)*, nutria *(Myocastor coypus)*, river otter *(Lutra canadensis)*, and beaver *(Castor canadensis)* (Schmidly 1983, 1984). All of the above species are rather common on the site with the exception of the river otter, which is present in unknown numbers. Feral hogs are extant throughout the project area and are hunted. These introduced animals damage vegetation because they root up plants searching for food.

Other characteristic bottomland mammal species likely to occur on the site include the marsh rice rat *(Oryzomys palustris)*, cotton mouse *(Peromyscus gossypinus)*, short-tailed shrew *(Blarina carolinensis)*, least shrew *(Cryptotis parve)*, eastern wood rat *(Neotoma floridana)*, and eastern mole *(Scalopus aquaticus)*.

Reptiles and Amphibians

A total of 54 species of reptiles and 31 species of amphibians are known to occur in bottomland hardwoods and associated wetland habitats in east Texas. This list includes 17 turtles; 1 crocodilian, the American alligator; 8 lizards; 28 snakes; 11 salamanders; and 20 toads and frogs (Fish and Wildlife Service 1985).

Characteristic reptiles and amphibians of the east Texas floodplains include the common snapping turtle *(Chelydra serpentina)*, alligator snapping turtle *(Macroclemys temmincki)*, red-eared slider *(Chrysemys scripta)*, the soft-shell turtles *(Trionyx* spp.), the water snakes *(Nerodia* spp.), western mud snake *(Farancia abacura)*, rat snake *(Elaphe obsoleta)*, cottonmouth *(Agkistrodon piscivorus)*, copperhead *(Agkistrodon contortrix)*, Canebrake rattlesnake *(Crotalus horridus)*, lesser siren *(Siren intermedia)*, tree frog *(Rana utricularia)*.

Fish

A total of 116 species of fish occur within east Texas. Many of these fish utilize bottomlands during seasonal inundation of the floodplain. The fish species that most commonly use the floodplain during periods of overflow flooding include the bowfin *(Amia calva)*, American eel *(Anquilla rostrata)*, red fin pickerel *(Esox americanus)*, chain pickerel *(Esox niger)*, yellow bullhead *(Ictalurus Natatlis)*, topminnows *(Fundulus* spp.), mosquito fish *(Gambusia affinis)*, Sunfish *(Lepomis* spp.), Flier *(Centrarchus macropterus)*, and swamp darter *(Etheostoma fusiforme)* (Wharton et al. 1982). Many of these species are believed to occur in the Neches River and its tributaries, but a fishery survey on the project site has yet to be conducted.

Invertebrates

There are a myriad of invertebrate species in the rivers, creeks, and floodplains in east Texas. Invertebrates are essential dietary components for a number of vertebrates previously discussed including the mallard and wood duck.

Animals of Special Concern

A number of animal species of special concern are known or believed to occur on the Neches River project area (Texas Organization for Endangered Species 1984; Texas Parks and Wildlife Department 1987a, b; and Fish and Wildlife Service 1987).

A colony of federally endangered red-cockaded woodpeckers has been documented in the I.D. Fairchild State Forest east of the project area.

The federally threatened American alligator is found in aquatic and wetland situations including major river drainages, creeks, marshes, swamps, lakes, and farm ponds, and is known to occur on the site. The American alligator is listed because of its similarity in appearance to the federally endangered American crocodile.

Some Texas biologists believe federally endangered Louisiana black bears are reintroducing themselves into suitable available habitat in their historic former East Texas range and are slowly expanding westward, but it is unlikely that they have reached the project area at this time.

The wood stork *(Mycteria americana)*, listed as a protected non-game species by the Texas Parks and Wildlife Department, is a migrant colonial water bird that utilizes swamps and other wetlands in east Texas during late summer. The wood stork was a former nester in southeast Texas swamps. Wood storks may occur at the site in late summer.

The osprey *(Pandion haliaetus)*, listed as a protected non-game species by the Texas Parks and Wildlife Department, is an uncommon migrant and winter visitor that utilizes a variety of aquatic situations and is a seasonal visitor in the area.

The federally-listed threatened bald eagle is a very rare nesting species in east Texas and uncommon on the Texas coast. This species has recently been on the increase and may winter on the project site. These birds characteristically nest in Texas along rivers and wooded lakeshores.

The river otter, listed as threatened by the Texas Organization for Endangered Species, seems to be increasing recently and is found in a variety of floodplain situations throughout east Texas. River otters are believed to occur along water bodies within the project area.

It is not known if the federal candidate species Louisiana pine snake is in the project area.

Land Use

Anderson County contains about 1,078 square miles, or 689,920 acres, in area. Cherokee County contains about 1,062 square miles, or 679,680 acres, in area (2004 Texas Almanac). The area for both counties combined is 1,369,600 acres.

Much of the project area is in the 100-year floodplain of the Neches River. The bottomlands are predominantly in mixed deciduous and conifer forests, shrub swamps and open water. The primary historical land use has been timber management for the wood products industry. Another prominent land use has been oil and gas drilling. Much of the private land has been leased for hunting, either to individuals or to clubs, and has provided an additional means of income for landowners.

The bluffs and uplands within the study area are rural and include forested lands and lands cleared for pastures and croplands, tree farms, or residences. There is also some oil and gas drilling in both the bottom lands and the uplands. Two major highways, 79 and 84, and several smaller rural access roads cross the study area. Two railroads cross the study area—the Union Pacific Railroad north of Highway 79 and the Texas State Railroad south of Highway 84.

Visitor Uses and Recreational Opportunities

About 40,000 people per year ride the Texas State Railroad through the study area on tracks located south of Highway 84. People enjoy both the experience of riding historic railroads and viewing the forested scenery along the tracks.

Hunting and fishing are the other primary recreational pursuits in the study area. The tradition and culture of leased hunting is strong here. Both large hunt clubs and numerous individual leases have existed in the project area for many years. Hunting lessees effectively keep the public from entering their lease areas, except when the landowner specifically allows or escorts such visitors. In recent years, some new landowners of large tracts have evicted all hunting lessees and suspended hunting lease programs.

In the 1980's, the Texas Parks and Wildlife Department started a program called Type II for public hunting access to private lands. Unfortunately, some of the hunters didn't always respect adjacent property lines (or they were not marked) and incidences of trespassing, littering, and vandalism have been reported by current landowners.

There are some public boat access sites on the river, mainly at Highway 84. The entire study area river reach is not fully navigable for recreational boaters due to beaver dams, logjams, and marshy areas, although there are stretches of the river that can be canoed.

Cultural Resources

Cultural resources include both archeological (pre-historic) and historic sites, structures, artifacts, remains and other tangible evidence of past cultures. The wet and mild climate of the project area promotes both rapid deterioration of structures, and dense vegetation growth that can potentially hide remnants of cultural resources. The known catalog of such resources is limited in the study area. However, many cultures were present throughout the years that undoubtedly contributed to the cultural resources within the area.

The Clovis, Caddo, and Cherokee tribes were present in prehistoric times in the project area. They were undoubtedly drawn to the availability of game and fish found in the river bottoms. There may be archeological resources from these native cultures within the study area.

European influences of Spanish and French missionaries, fur trappers, and soldiers within the area may indicate possible historic resources in the study area. There may also be remnants of later Anglo historic settlements within the area as well. A number of historic sawmill sites from the late 1800's to the early 1900's may occur within the study area.

Nearby towns such as Palestine are known for their historic homes and downtown areas that attract many visitors.

Alternative Land Use Proposals Undergoing Study

In order to perform the requisite "due diligence" toward compliance with the National Environmental Policy Act of 1969, the Service must consider its refuge proposal within the light of public discussions relative to other potential uses for the area. Therefore, it is only prudent to disclose that the Service has been made aware that the area under consideration was identified in a preliminary study by the Texas Water Plan as an area with the potential for development as a reservoir to act as water supply for the Dallas metro-plex. More recently, a resolution is under consideration by the City of Dallas to develop a feasibility study for the eventual development of a reservoir along the north Neches River. The City anticipates that such a study would entail hydrological assessment, costs, scope and impacts of such a proposal. Because the Service considers this project far beyond the planning horizon for the refuge proposal, it cannot do any more than speculate as to how the two projects would interface. As such a proposal moves closer to possible implementation, it is important to note that should there be a refuge in place (i.e. tracts of land under title to the United States), that coincides with the geographical footprint of a reservoir, there would need to be an under standing that the Service is not authorized to divest of lands with the Refuge System. It is likely that the Service and the City of Dallas will have to develop each of the respective proposals with intent to be collaborative when possible.

Socioeconomic Resources and Regional Socioeconomic Context

County	County Road Lane Miles 2003	Geographic Size (sq mi)	Population Density 2003 (people/sq mi)	Tax Rate 2003	Total Appraised Value 2003	Total Taxable Value 2003	Total Population 2003 (Est.)	Zoom To County	Highlight County	MSA Info (SA = Statistical Area)
Anderson	1,723.51	1,071	52	0.46686	$2,281,815,970.00	$1,690,853,115	56,006	Anderson	Anderson	Palestine, TX Micropolitan SA
Cherokee	1,887.19	1,052	46	0.6	$1,825,483,414.00	$1,360,603,372	47,883	Cherokee	Cherokee	Jacksonville, TX Micropolitan SA

For additional information or comments, contact Tim Brown, Operations Manager of the County Information Project. Development by *wptc, Inc.*, Austin Texas

Comparative Table (data as of 2003)

Anderson County is a county located in the state of Texas. As of 2000, the population is 55,109. Its county seat is Palestine[6]. Anderson county was organized in 1846, and is named in honor of Kenneth L. Anderson who had been Vice President of the Republic of Texas. According to the U.S. Census Bureau, the county has a total area of 2,792 km² (1,078 mi²). 2,773 km² (1,071 mi²) of it is land and 19 km² (7 mi²) of it is water. The total area is 0.66% water.

Palestine (pronounced PAL-es-teen) is a city located in Anderson County, Texas. As of the 2000 census, the city had a total population of 17,598. It is the county seat of Anderson County[6] and is situated in East Texas. Palestine was named for Palestine, Illinois, the home of an early settler. It is the home of the National Scientific Balloon Facility. Palestine entered the news in February, 2003, as one of the East Texas towns that received much of the Space Shuttle Columbia disaster debris.

Cherokee County is a county located in the state of Texas. As of 2000, the population is 46,659. Its county seat is Rusk[6]. Cherokee is named for the Cherokee Native American Tribe. According to the U.S. Census Bureau, the county has a total area of 2,750 km² (1,062 mi²). 2,725 km² (1,052 mi²) of it is land and 25 km² (10 mi²) of it is water. The total area is 0.92% water.

Jacksonville is a city located in Cherokee County, Texas. As of the 2000 census, the city had a total population of 13,868.

Jacksonville is located in an area of rolling hills in East Texas, north of the county seat, Rusk, and south of Tyler, in Smith County, on U. S. Highway 69. Area production and shipping of tomatoes gained the town the title "Tomato Capital of the World". Annual events include the "Tomato Fest" celebration in June, and the "Tops in Texas Rodeo", held in July.

Jacksonville began in 1847 as the town of Gum Creek. Jackson Smith built a home and blacksmith shop in the area, and became postmaster in 1848, when a post office was authorized. Shortly afterward, Dr. William Jackson established an office near Smith's shop. When the townsite was laid out in 1850, the name Jacksonville was chosen in honor of these two men. The name of the post office was changed from Gum Creek to Jacksonville in June of 1850.

Texas' only two privately owned junior colleges - Lon Morris and Jacksonville College - are both located in Jacksonville. A seminary belonging to the Baptist Missionary Association of America is also located there.

Cherokee County Demographics

As of the census[2] of 2000, there are 46,659 people, 16,651 households, and 12,105 families residing in the county. The population density is 17/km² (44/mi²). There are 19,173 housing units at an average density of 7/km² (18/mi²). The racial makeup of the county is 74.34% White, 15.96% Black or African American, 0.47% Native American,

0.40% Asian, 0.06% Pacific Islander, 7.43% from other races, and 1.34% from two or more races. 13.24% of the population are Hispanic or Latino of any race.

There are 16,651 households out of which 33.40% have children under the age of 18 living with them, 55.70% are married couples living together, 12.80% have a female householder with no husband present, and 27.30% are non-families. 24.20% of all households are made up of individuals and 11.90% have someone living alone who is 65 years of age or older. The average household size is 2.63 and the average family size is 3.11.

In the county, the population is spread out with 26.30% under the age of 18, 9.30% from 18 to 24, 27.40% from 25 to 44, 21.90% from 45 to 64, and 15.10% who are 65 years of age or older. The median age is 36 years. For every 100 females there are 101.00 males. For every 100 females age 18 and over, there are 99.00 males.

The median income for a household in the county is $29,313, and the median income for a family is $34,750. Males have a median income of $26,410 versus $19,788 for females. The per capita income for the county is $13,980. 17.90% of the population and 13.70% of families are below the poverty line. Out of the total population, 23.30% of those under the age of 18 and 15.10% of those 65 and older are living below the poverty line.

Anderson County Demographics

As of the census[2] of 2000, there are 55,109 people, 15,678 households, and 11,335 families residing in the county. The population density is 20/km² (52/mi²). There are 18,436 housing units at an average density of 7/km² (17/mi²). The racial makeup of the county is 66.44% White, 23.48% Black or African American, 0.64% Native American, 0.45% Asian, 0.03% Pacific Islander, 8.00% from other races, and 0.96% from two or more races. 12.17% of the population are Hispanic or Latino of any race.

There are 15,678 households out of which 34.10% have children under the age of 18 living with them, 55.50% are married couples living together, 13.20% have a female householder with no husband present, and 27.70% are non-families. 24.80% of all households are made up of individuals and 11.80% have someone living alone who is 65 years of age or older. The average household size is 2.58 and the average family size is 3.07.

In the county, the population is spread out with 20.70% under the age of 18, 9.30% from 18 to 24, 37.70% from 25 to 44, 20.60% from 45 to 64, and 11.70% who are 65 years of age or older. The median age is 36 years. For every 100 females there are 155.80 males. For every 100 females age 18 and over, there are 173.40 males.

The median income for a household in the county is $31,957, and the median income for a family is $37,513. Males have a median income of $27,070 versus $21,577 for females. The per capita income for the county is $13,838. 16.50% of the population and 12.70% of families are below the poverty line. Out of the total population, 21.60% of those under the age of 18 and 16.60% of those 65 and older are living below the poverty line.

IV. ENVIRONMENTAL CONSEQUENCES

Alternative A: No Action

This alternative would mean that the status quo would be maintained; essentially allowing present land uses and trends to continue within the project area.

Alternative A: Effects on Climate and Air Quality

This alternative would have no significant effect on climate, which results from global conditions.

Alternative A: Effects on Geology and Soils

This alternative would not significantly affect geological features and soils.

Since third parties hold many of the mineral estates in the project area, this alternative should have no impact on minerals development or extraction in the expansion area. Mining is not now a significant economic sector in the project area and would likely not become one in the future.

As anticipated development proceeds in the area, soils will be disturbed on developed sites. Without measures to protect soils, such as silt curtains or revegetation, this may lead to increased erosion and siltation into water bodies.

Alternative A: Effects on Water Resources

Under this alternative there may be some increased siltation into the Neches River and its tributaries as a result of soil disturbances from anticipated development in the area. The degree of effect would depend on the type of development and its proximity to any water bodies.

The problem of flooded oil drilling facilities located in the bottom lands will likely continue to affect water quality.

In the long term, the Fastrill Dam and Reservoir could eventually be built if it is economically feasible. The specific location of the full reservoir foot print is not yet known. Depending upon hydrological factors, the general location of a dam site, the reservoir pool could submerge an area encompassing approximately 25,000 acres. It is likely that the level of inundation would destroy all vegetation in the floodplain. If such a reservoir is to be built, it is likely that it would be sponsored by the City of Dallas Metroplex.

Alternative A: Effects on Vegetation

Forested uplands could be logged or cleared in the future for potential residential development, new pastures, or tree farms.

The current trend of timber company land divestiture will likely continue in the short term. In the long term, expected increased world demand for wood products may provide incentives to log the bottomlands. Clearing for development in the bottomlands is still not likely to occur because it is located in a flood plain.

Alternative A: Effects on Fish and Wildlife

In the short term, fish and wildlife resources would likely continue with current population trends. Since much of the bottomlands are in the Neches River floodplain, significant increased development causing habitat degradation would not be anticipated. Leased hunting would likely continue on many tracts. However, some illegal hunting is known to occur in the area, which may have adverse impacts on some species' populations.

Alternative A: Effects on Land Use

A large percentage of the lands within the proposed refuge (per Alternative B) are owned by forest product corporations. (i.e. 85%) The trend among the nation's large forest product corporations has been toward divesture of land holdings, and this is already happening in the project area. Real estate investment companies and insurance companies have been frequent buyers of these large tracts. Future owners may consider logging their tracts because increased world demand for wood products may provide an incentive for logging.

Rural residential and agricultural development would likely continue in the upland areas above the river floodplain.

Oil and gas drilling would likely continue as long as the petroleum resource is available and world oil prices support continued drilling.

A natural gas pipeline is anticipated to be built soon through the study area. At least four other pipelines and one major utility line cross the river within the project area. Development of new utility rights of way and pipelines could occur in the future.

Alternative A: Effects on Public Use and Recreation

In the short term, current recreational activities would likely continue. Hunting and fishing remain popular outdoor recreational pursuits in this part of Texas. Hunting leases would likely continue in the short term on tracts with existing leases. As lands change hands in the future, new landowners may, or may not, continue that use depending on their preferences and financial situations.

The public is generally not allowed on private lands within the study area. Hunting clubs prohibit entry onto their leases by the public. There are limited public boating and fishing access points on the river.

The Texas State Railroad would likely continue its operations, as long as the State can afford to support that endeavor, and it remains popular. At this time, the railroad is the only way for most of the public to view the Neches River bottomlands.

Alternative A: Effects on Cultural Resources

Protection of cultural resources would be an optional action by private landowners. The National Historic Preservation Act does not require cultural resource protection on private lands. Voluntary participation in any cooperative conservation program would remain within the sole discretion of the private landowner. It is likely that any sites that may be present would continue to deteriorate in the humid, warm climate of the region.

Alternative A: Effects on Socioeconomic Resources

Under the No Action Alternative, it is likely that the area would continue to remain rural in character and it is likely that current economic uses of the land (i.e. forest products) would continue fluctuating with the market.

Alternative A: Effects on the Local Tax Base

An analysis is being conducted and will be an addendum to this document within 20 days from the release of this document.

Alternative B: Proposed boundary encompassing approximately 25,281 acres

Alternative B: Effects on Climate and Air Quality

Since 25,281 acres is a relatively small portion of the air shed within the more than 1,369,000 acres in the project's combined two-county area, land acquisition will not appreciably affect overall air quality. However, protection of a continuous stand of bottomland forest from future loss would contribute to climate maintenance and air quality through carbon sequestration which reduces ozone production and other air pollutants.

Alternative B: Effects on Geology and Soils

Establishment of the Refuge would allow continued oil and gas drilling. Most mineral rights are held by third parties or would most likely be reserved by landowners who sell or donate lands or easements. Refuge managers would work cooperatively with drilling operators to minimize adverse environmental effects of drilling on Refuge lands.

Alternative B: Effects on Water Resources

Establishment of the Refuge and subsequent acquisition of lands in fee or easement would prevent the development of the Fastrill Reservoir because federal lands generally cannot be subjugated by any local or state project.

The Refuge would not prevent the continued diversion of river water for Palestine from the current point of diversion.

Alternative B: Effects on Vegetation

The Refuge would manage the bottomland forests for native species diversity in support of wildlife management goals. The forests would be managed in line with sustainable management. Clear cutting of healthy native tree stands, especially mast (fruit) producing hardwoods would not be practiced. The Service would keep native evergreen species and would strive to replace introduced loblolly pine or slash pine species with native hardwoods or evergreens, depending on what was better suited to the site.

The Refuge would maintain sandy prairie sites for the native vegetation present, especially the sites that contain species of concern, such as the *Geocarpum minimum.*

Alternative B: Effects on Fish and Wildlife

An Intra-Service Section 7 Biological Evaluation Form was prepared for this proposed action. A Section 7 (referring to Section 7 of the Endangered Species Act of 1973, as amended) biological evaluation is required for all major Federal actions. The Service's Ft. Worth Ecological Services Office concurred with the Intra-Service Section 7 Biological Evaluation determination on October 14, 2004 that establishment of the refuge up to 25,281 acres would have no adverse effect on federally-listed threatened, endangered, or candidate species. (Appendix 6)

As on other refuges in the southeast part of the country, managers would have a feral hog management program. Hogs would be removed whenever possible.

Alternative B: Effects on Land Use

A twenty-five thousand-acre refuge would encompass 1.8 percent of the total acreage in the two counties.

The Service would manage the bottomland forests for native species diversity in support of wildlife management goals. Timber harvests that support those goals could occur, if a forest management prescription warranted that action. Large-scale timber cutting of the bottomland hardwoods would not be practiced.

The Service is required to survey any potential acquisition for the presence of contaminants, or hazardous materials, or other hazardous conditions such as abandoned open water wells. Since only rural properties are generally acquired, typical considerations include household and farm chemicals, small household dumps, and above-ground or underground fuel storage tanks. Oil and gas drilling structures including wells, tank batteries, overflow pits, and gathering lines would also be surveyed. Since these are often owned by third parties and not in control of the surface landowners, the Service would consider if any contaminant problems can be resolved, or if not, reconsider acquiring the property.

The Service accommodates utility rights-of-way, pipelines, and oil drilling operations of third parties having mineral property rights on its refuges, and would continue to do so if the Refuge is established. Those wanting to build such infrastructures on lands already purchased by the United States would apply for special use permits from the refuge manager. Refuge managers typically work with applicants to minimize any adverse environmental effects of infrastructure developments. The Service cannot deny mineral owners reasonable access to their mineral rights. Infrastructure development on private in-holdings or adjacent private properties would not be affected.

Alternative B: Effects on Public Use and Recreation

The Service would develop compatible public recreational opportunities on lands acquired in fee. The public would be able to visit some Neches River bottomlands that were previously inaccessible. The Service would try to maximize opportunities for compatible public recreation on acquired fee lands. Refuge managers often reserve some areas for sanctuary so that wildlife can have some security for resting, feeding, and breeding. Until acquired lands can be evaluated, it cannot be determined at this time where and what specific visitor use facilities or wildlife sanctuary areas will be set up.

The Conceptual Management Plan (appended to this EA) outlines refuge visitor recreation opportunities that could be made available on suitable tracts acquired in fee. Lands acquired with a conservation/access/management easement may not be available for public use, as the landowner generally retains the right to exclude the public. It would also be up to the landowner to retain or institute a hunting lease program on conservation easement lands.

The Service would inventory roads on acquired tracts. Some refuge tracts may have limited, primarily unimproved, existing road access. Areas such as these would typically have primitive access only, especially in the frequently flooded bottomlands

Hunting could be allowed on certain acquired tracts that are large enough to accommodate hunters without causing disturbance to adjacent land owners, especially tracts with large expanses of interior forest. Smaller, isolated properties may not be large enough for a quality hunting experience or ensure the safety of adjacent landowners.

Establishment of a refuge would not adversely affect the Texas State Railroad's historic tourist train trips through the Neches River bottomlands. If the lands the Railroad goes through were acquired for the Refuge, it would be one way for people to see the Refuge. At current rider-ship, about 40,000 people ride the Railroad annually. The presence of the rail road resource presents an opportunity for both the State of Texas and the Service to jointly develop an interpretive program for scenic, wildlife related resources along the railway line.

In the meantime, the Service, by policy is required to develop Interim Compatibility Determinations for an array of priority public uses. Those draft determinations are attached to this document as Appendix 5. Following the approval of the Refuge establishment proposal by the Service Director, those Interim Compatibility Determinations will be made final.

Alternative B: Effects on Cultural Resources

The Service, as are all other federal agencies, is required to protect cultural resources on all acquired lands under Section 106 of the National Historic Preservation Act of 1966, the Archeological Resources Protection Act of 1979 and the Antiquities Act of 1906 by consulting with the Texas Historical Commission regarding the protection of any potential cultural resource sites on specific properties proposed for acquisition. If any archaeological or historical resources are acquired in the expanded area, refuge management activities are supposed to protect or minimize impact on such resources. If cultural resources are found during construction of any Refuge facility, the Service is required to salvage or protect those resources. For those lands remaining in private ownership, it is a voluntary consideration by the private landowner to ensure protection of these resources.

Alternative B: Effects on Socioeconomic Resources

Generally, the presence of a National Wildlife Refuge has positive effects on the local economy as it will introduce some additional employment and purchasing of resources from the local economy. The expectation is that as the refuge develops and grows, that it would undoubtedly contribute to an already growing ecotourism economic base in the State of Texas. Generally refuges and their staffs contribute strongly in assisting local Chambers of Commerce and the local educational systems to promote the long lasting intrinsic values inherent in the Refuge System and its wildlife and habitat resources. This is the larger of the alternatives and would provide more diversity of habitats to interpret and present in the development of informational kiosks, auto tour routes and interpretive trails.

Alternative B: Effects on Local Tax Base

An analysis is being conducted and will be an addendum to the Environmental Assessment within 20 days from the release of this document.

Alternative C: Proposed boundary encompassing approximately 15,294 acres

Alternative C: Effects on Climate and Air Quality

Since 15,294 acres is a small portion of the air shed over more than 1,369,000 acres in the project's two-county area, land acquisition will not appreciably affect overall air quality. However, protection of a continuous stand of bottomland forest from future loss would contribute to climate maintenance and air quality through carbon sequestration which reduces ozone production and other air pollutants.

Alternative C: Effects on Geology and Soils

Establishment of the Refuge in a river corridor only scenario would allow continued oil and gas drilling because most mineral rights are held by third parties or would most likely be reserved by landowners who might sell or donate lands or easements. Refuge managers would work cooperatively with drilling operators to minimize adverse environmental effects of drilling on Refuge lands.

Alternative C: Effects on Water Resources

As with Alternative B, this alternative of establishment of the Refuge and subsequent acquisition of lands in fee or easement would prevent the development of a Water Reservoir because federal lands generally cannot be dominated by any local or state project. The Refuge would not prevent the continued diversion of river water for Palestine from the current point of diversion.

Alternative C: Effects on Vegetation

Effects on vegetation from this smaller alternative would be similar to Alternative B, except that this alternative provides protection to plant communities mainly in the riparian corridor and does not include many of the tracts containing pine plantation.

Alternative C: Effects on Fish and Wildlife

This smaller alternative would provide protection for habitats mainly in the flood plain areas within the riparian corridor closest to the bottomland vegetation. Any vegetation restoration that may be possible with acquisition of cleared areas could enhance the habitat values of the riparian corridor for those species that need more cover.

Alternative C: Effects on Land Use

This smaller alternative reduces the number of acres in both Anderson and Cherokee Counties. Most of the lands include wetlands and floodplain areas containing the oldest and largest stands of bottom lands. The intent of the layout of this alternative was to focus primarily on the protection of the hardwood resources as opposed to areas containing pine plantation. Current owners do not harvest these resources but future owners may decide to. When conservation easements are sold to the Service, it is likely that hunting lease rights will continue for those lands. For those bottomlands purchased in fee by the United States, private leases will cease.

Alternative C: Effects on Public Use and Recreation

This alternative is different from Alternative B in size and scope. There would be fewer upland areas available for hunting and wildlife observation activities (i.e. potential development sites for overlooks and interpretive trails. The Service would implement any public use and recreation program to avoid any adverse effects on adjacent land owners in the area. Otherwise, the effects on visitor use and recreation are essentially the same as those of Alternative B.

Alternative C: Effects on Cultural Resources

The Service, as are all other federal agencies, is required to protect cultural resources on all acquired lands under Section 106 of the National Historic Preservation Act of 1966, the Archeological Resources Protection Act of 1979 and the Antiquities Act of 1906 by consulting with the Texas Historical Commission regarding the protection of any potential cultural resource sites on specific properties proposed for acquisition. If any archaeological or historical resources are acquired in this reduced area, refuge management activities are supposed to protect or minimize impact on such resources. If cultural resources are found during construction of any Refuge facility, the Service is required to salvage or protect those resources. For those lands remaining in private ownership, it is a voluntary consideration by the private landowner to ensure protection of these resources.

Alternative C: Effects on Socioeconomic Resources

Generally, the presence of a National Wildlife Refuge has positive effects on the local economy as it will introduce some additional employment and purchasing of resources from the local economy. The expectation is that as the refuge develops and grows, that it would undoubtedly contribute to an already growing ecotourism economic base in the State of Texas. Generally refuges and their staffs contribute strongly in assisting local Chambers of Commerce and the local educational systems to promote the long lasting intrinsic values inherent in the Refuge System and its wildlife and habitat resources. This is the smaller of the alternatives and would provide less diversity of habitats to interpret and present in the development of informational kiosks, auto tour routes and interpretive trails.

Alternative C: Effects on Local Tax Base

An analysis is being conducted and will be an addendum to this document within 20 days from the release of this document.

V. CUMULATIVE IMPACTS

Cumulative impacts are those that result from the incremental impacts of the action when added to other past, present, and reasonably foreseeable future actions. Therefore, the impacts of the proposed Neches River National Wildlife Refuge need to be measured against the impacts of other federal land protection actions. There are 19 other national wildlife refuges in Texas, currently including almost 600,000 acres.

Acquisitions would be limited by future funding and the existence of willing sellers. If the refuge expanded to the full 25,281 acres, it would take up 1.8 percent of the total acreage in Anderson and Cherokee Counties. This would not entail a significant impact on any resource or issue of the affected environment.

The presence of a national wildlife refuge would require that a larger water reservoir be planned so that any overlap with refuge resources would be minimized. Non establishment of a refuge would most likely mean that water planning could develop the reservoir over a significant portion of the project area thereby inundating the bottom land hardwood resources in need of protection. If the proposed Fastrill Reservoir is constructed, about 25,000 acres of bottomland habitats would be flooded, significantly decreasing those species affected. A reservoir would effectively eliminate a link of the river's riparian corridor needed by many animals to move throughout their ranges along the river's reach. Should the State of Texas build a water reservoir, land uses in the former bottomlands would change. Development of the reservoir could necessitate the use of eminent domain authority by the State of Texas on lands within the proposed reservoir pool. Residential and water related recreational development would likely be a strong eventual presence along the shores of the reservoir.

VI. CONSULTATION AND COORDINATION

The Fish and Wildlife Service officially introduced the study for the proposed Neches River National Wildlife Refuge to the public in June 2004. This phase of the detailed study was the scoping phase—determining the important issues to be analyzed in the environmental assessment for potential impacts of the proposal. Before the proposal went public, elected officials including U.S. senators, U.S. Congressional representatives, state senators, state representatives, and county judges were notified of the proposal by letter. The Service developed a database of landowners within the overall study boundary obtained from the Anderson County Assessor's Office and the Cherokee County Appraisal District. Those landowners were then notified of the proposal by letter in July 2004. There were some gaps in the ownership data, or some obsolete entries in the 2-3-year-old data, so that a few landowners were not reached, unless they notified the Service of that occurrence. The Service announced that two scoping workshops would be held on July 20 and 21, 2004, to provide information on the proposal, answer questions, and elicit the affected stakeholders' issues and concerns about the proposed refuge. Other parties were also specifically notified such as Texas Parks and Wildlife Department, the two county Farm Bureau presidents, and the Texas State Railroad.

As the scoping phase continued throughout the summer and fall of 2004, more affected stakeholders came forward, or were identified by the Service. These included the East Texas Regional Water Planning Group. A presentation, including a question and answer forum, was given on October 13, 2004, in Nacogdoches to this organization and interested members of the public.

This environmental assessment, land protection plan and draft concept management plan will be distributed to public officials, affected federal, state, and local agencies, non profit conservation organizations, academic institutions, affected landowners, and individuals who have expressed an interest in the refuge. These documents will undergo a 60-day public review before a final decision is made on the refuge establishment proposal. Reviewers are encouraged to forward their comments via letter, fax, or e-mail to the U.S. Fish and Wildlife Service, Division of Planning, P.O. Box 1306, Albuquerque, New Mexico 87103; or fax: 505-248-6874; or e-mail: tom_baca@fws.gov.

LAND PROTECTION PLAN FOR NORTH NECHES RIVER NWR

Project Description

The U.S. Fish and Wildlife Service (Service) proposes to establish the Neches River National Wildlife Refuge in Anderson and Cherokee Counties, Texas. The proposed refuge could include up to 25,281 acres. Habitats would be protected by acquiring lands in fee title or in conservation/access/management easements at fair market value from willing sellers and donors.

Status of Resources To Be Protected

In 1985 the Fish and Wildlife Service identified this reach of the Neches River as important in its Texas Bottomland Hardwood Concept Plan and in its Land Protection Plan for Bottomland Hardwoods, Category 3, Texas and Oklahoma. The Service listed the "Neches River North" as a Priority 1 protection need.

In 1988, the Service Directorate approved the Preliminary Project Proposal to proceed in the development of more detailed planning for a 25,281 acre refuge in the upper Neches area. At that time, land costs were estimated at approximately $18 million. Those costs today would be approximately $33 million. The approval letter dated January 6, 1988, stated that the "waterfowl use numbers, when determined during the detailed planning phase, should determine whether Migratory Bird Conservation Funds, Land, and Water Conservation Funds, or a combination of both shall be the funding source for this unit." The proposal states:

> "The Neches River National Wildlife Refuge is being proposed to preserve bottom-land hardwoods that are important wintering habitat for mallards and wood ducks and production habitat for wood ducks. This proposal is designed to assist in meeting the habitat goals presented in the Ten-Year Waterfowl Habitat Acquisition Report (Category 3) and the North American Waterfowl Management Plan. The proposed area also protects a large number of other wildlife and plant species and will be of potential benefit to the federally endangered bald eagle and red-cockaded woodpecker, the threatened American Alligator, and several State species of special concern."

Proposed Action and Objective

The purposes of the proposed Neches River National Wildlife Refuge would be 1) protect nesting, wintering and migratory habitat for migratory birds of the Central Flyway, 2) to protect the bottomland hardwood forests for their diverse biological values and wetland functions of water quality improvement and flood control assistance, and 3) provide for compatible wildlife-dependent recreation opportunities.

Land Resource Protection Alternatives

No Action

This alternative includes the status quo, or what the Service and other entities are already doing, and would continue doing, if the proposed action was not started to protect habitats and species of concern, migratory birds, and the biological diversity of the north Neches River ecosystem.

Acquisition and/or Management by Others

This alternative assumes a commitment and effort by other federal and state agencies, non profit conservation organizations, and private landowners to protect bottomland hardwood forests along the Neches River. Although these other entities are making important contributions to protect vulnerable habitats, their financial and staff resources to acquire and manage properties are limited.

A number of private landowners are doing an exemplary job of managing their own properties with wildlife conservation and watershed protection in mind. However, properties kept in the private sector cannot be assured of perpetual protection. Subsequent heirs or owners may not always have the financial resources or commitment to follow through with long term protection.

United States (FWS) Acquisition of Interest in Land

Fee Title Interest in Land

Fee acquisition by the Service would provide permanent protection of the important bottom land hardwood resources identified along the Neches River NWR project area. Refuge managers would have complete freedom to manage those tracts as their management plans recommend. The Service would make annual payments to county governments, called refuge revenue sharing payments, to help offset the loss of property tax payments for those tracts acquired and taken off the tax rolls.

Conservation Easement Interest in Land

Conservation easements are often referred to as non-development easements. The buyer pays the landowner for the transfer of certain rights. Easement restrictions get recorded at the courthouse just like deeds and future landowners would be required to abide by those restrictions. The restrictions, however, usually lower the dollar value of the land. The landowner may sell or donate a perpetual (eternal) conservation easement to the Service and may receive income and estate tax benefits from the donation. The landowner still pays property taxes on the land, but does not have to allow public access to the land, unless he or she grants permission. The federal government would make no refuge revenue sharing payment to the county for conservation easements it holds.

The Service and the landowner would negotiate the exact terms of a conservation easement on a case by case basis for each tract. General terms of an easement would include acquisition of rights considered necessary to achieve habitat protection and/or management goals. The landowner would retain title to and occupation of the property. Property rights that could be acquired include, but are not limited to, the following:

- Development Rights—All types of surface development including, but not limited to, construction of buildings, roads, pipelines, power lines, or other structures.
- Disturbance of Vegetation Rights—Clearing or burning of any vegetation or other activities such as grazing, impoundment of water, or application of herbicides or other chemicals that could impact vegetation or wildlife.
- Right to Control Access—the right to control access to and/or through property.
- Water Rights—The right to use defined quantities of surface and/or subsurface water.
- Rights not acquired in the easement would remain with the landowner. The more rights the landowner grants, the more the purchase price approaches full fee value.

Easements may enable landowners who want to conserve their properties for wildlife, but who may not have the financial and technical resources, to do it. This alternative frees the Service from having to make revenue sharing payments on those tracts. If the landowner also resides on the tract, he serves as a more constant presence to discourage illegal activities by some visitors. Since the landowner is able to give or deny the public permission to enter the property, it also frees the Service from liability concerns, having to provide public use facilities, or monitor hunters and other recreational users. However, some landowners are not interested in selling or donating easements. They want to divest themselves of the property and/or they need the money from the sale of the property.

Public Involvement and Coordination

The Fish and Wildlife Service officially introduced the study for the proposed Neches River National Wildlife Refuge to the public in June 2004. This phase of the detailed study was the scoping phase—determining the important issues to be analyzed in the environmental assessment for potential impacts of the proposal. Before the proposal went public, elected officials including U.S. senators, U.S. Congressional representatives, state senators, state representatives, and county judges were notified of the proposal by letter. The Service developed a database of landowners within the overall study boundary obtained from the Anderson County Assessor's Office and the Cherokee County Appraisal District. Those landowners were then notified of the proposal by letter in July 2004. There were some gaps in the ownership data, or some obsolete entries in the 2-3-year-old data, so that a few landowners were not reached, unless they notified the Service of that occurrence. The Service announced that two scoping workshops would be held on July 20 and 21, 2004, to provide information on the proposal, answer questions, and elicit the affected stakeholders' issues and concerns about the proposed refuge. Other parties were also specifically notified such as Texas Parks and Wildlife Department, the two county Farm Bureau presidents, and the Texas State Railroad.

As the scoping phase continued throughout the summer and fall of 2004, more affected stakeholders came forward, or were identified by the Service. These included the East Texas Regional Water Planning Group. A presentation, including a question and answer forum was given on October 13, 2004, in Nacogdoches to this organization and interested members of the public.

This environmental assessment, land protection plan and concept management plan will be distributed to public officials, affected federal, state, and local agencies, non profit conservation organizations, academic institutions, affected landowners, and individuals who have expressed an interest in the refuge. These documents will undergo a 45-day public review before a final decision is made on the boundary expansion proposal. Reviewers are encouraged to forward their comments via letter, fax, or e-mail to the U.S. Fish and Wildlife Service, Division of Planning, P.O. Box 1306, Albuquerque, New Mexico 87103; or fax: 505-248-6874; or e-mail: tom_baca@fws.gov.

CONCEPTUAL MANAGEMENT PLAN FOR NORTH NECHES RIVER NWR

I. Introduction

This conceptual management plan for a national wildlife refuge that the Service might establish for the Neches River National Wildlife Refuge within Anderson and Cherokee Counties in Texas presents a general outline on how those tracts would be managed. The lands discussed would be purchased from willing sellers (fee title), accepted as donations, or managed through conservation easements or agreements. As a conceptual plan, it does not provide extensive detail, pinpoint exactly where facilities would be, or show exactly where public use facilities would be located. Those details will be included in a formal refuge comprehensive conservation plan (CCP) with input from the public and in accordance with the National Environmental Policy Act. The CCP addresses the compatibility requirements in the National Wildlife Refuge System Administrative Act as amended by the National Wildlife Refuge System Improvement Act, and the Refuge Recreation Act. All management and public use actions must be compatible with the purposes for which a refuge is established. However, this plan should answer those questions commonly posed by the public during the planning and public involvement process for consideration of establishing a new national wildlife refuge.

II. Mission and Goals of the National Wildlife Refuge System

With the passage of the National Wildlife Refuge System Improvement Act of 1997, the mission of the National Wildlife Refuge System " . . . is to administer a national network of lands and waters for the conservation, management, and where appropriate, restoration of the fish, wildlife, and plant resources and their habitats within the United States for the benefit of present and future generations of Americans."

Refuge System Goals. The Fish and Wildlife Service Director's Order No. 132 states the following goals to guide the administration, management, and growth of the system:

- To fulfill our statutory duty to achieve refuge purpose(s) and further the System mission.
- Conserve, restore where appropriate, and enhance all species of fish, wildlife, and plants that are endangered or threatened with becoming endangered.
- Perpetuate migratory bird, inter-jurisdictional fish, and marine mammal populations.
- Conserve a diversity of fish, wildlife, and plants.
- Conserve and restore, where appropriate, representative ecosystems of the United States, including the ecological processes characteristic of those ecosystems.

- To foster understanding and instill appreciation of fish, wildlife, and plants, and their conservation, by providing the public with safe, high quality, and compatible wildlife-dependent public use. Such use includes hunting, fishing, wildlife observation and photography, and environmental education and interpretation.

Purposes of Proposed Neches River National Wildlife Refuge. Refuge purpose statements are primary to the management of each refuge within the System. The purpose statement along with the Mission of the NWRS are the bases upon which primary management activities are determined. These statements are the foundation from which "allowed" uses of refuges are determined through a defined "compatibility" process.

The purposes of the proposed Neches River National Wildlife Refuge would be 1) protect nesting, wintering and migratory habitat for migratory birds of the Central Flyway, 2) to protect the bottomland hardwood forests for their diverse biological values and wetland functions of water quality improvement and flood control assistance, and 3) provide for compatible wildlife-dependent recreation opportunities. These purposes would be cited specifically as:

> ... For use as an inviolate sanctuary, or for any other management purpose, for migratory birds. 16 U.S.C. sec. 715d (Migratory Bird Conservation Act)

> ... the conservation of the wetlands of the Nation in order to maintain the public benefits they provide and to help fulfill international obligations contained in various migratory bird treaties and conventions ... 16 U.S.C. sec. 3901(b), 100 Stat. 3583 (Emergency Wetlands Resources Act of 1986)

> "... For the development, advancement, management, conservation, and protection of fish and wildlife resources ..." 16 U.S.C. sec. 742f (a)(4) "... for the benefit of the United States Fish and Wildlife Service, in performing its activities and services. Such acceptance may be subject to the terms of any restrictive or affirmative covenant, or condition of servitude ..." 16 U.S.C. sec. 742f(b)(1) (Fish and Wildlife Act of 1956)

III. Refuge Administration

If the Neches River National Wildlife Refuge is established it would become part of the National Wildlife Refuge System and would be subject to laws and policies applicable to units of the system.

Staffing. A new Neches River National Wildlife Refuge would become a unit of the Caddo Lake National Wildlife Refuge Complex whose offices are located in Harrison County, Texas. Initially, the Caddo Lake Refuge Manager would manage the Neches River NWR as the first lands are being acquired. Caddo Lake NWR also currently has a wildlife biologist. The refuge could host volunteers and occasional researchers.

Headquarters Location. Initially, the new refuge would have headquarters at the Caddo Lake NWR offices in Karnack, Harrison County, Texas. Refuge offices are generally open from 7:30 a.m. to 4:00 p.m., Monday through Friday.

Refuge Budget. The budget for a refuge covers salaries, construction material purchases, equipment purchase and maintenance, supplies, the fire management program, law enforcement expenses, endangered species recovery expenses, and special project funds. Much of these expenses would probably be initially absorbed by the Caddo Lake NWR complex which would share staff and other resources with the Neches River NWR. Refuge expansion to a full 25,000 acres could entail an increase in the refuge budget to cover additional salaries for a refuge biologist and a law enforcement officer—a reasonable staff complement for a new refuge. This would be estimated to cost about $280,000 in the first year, but would go down to about $128,000 in subsequent years. An estimated $250,000 in one-time costs would be needed in the long run to accomplish plant and animal surveys, perform Geographic Information Systems (GIS) mapping of refuge units, complete some land surveys, renovate buildings for refuge uses, and some lesser miscellaneous operating needs.

BREAKDOWN OF INITIAL AND SUBSEQUENT YEARS COSTS

PERSONNEL: (IN $)

GS-11 Biologist - Salary (FERS/benefits):		66,000
	PCS Move:	26,000
	Vehicle/ATV:	39,000
	Computer/IT:	7,000
	Office Furniture/Supplies:	7,000
GS-9 LEO -	Salary (FERS/benefits):	55,000
	PCS Move:	22,000
	Vehicle/ATV:	44,000
	Computer/IT:	7,000
	Office Furniture/Supplies:	7,000
Initial Year Costs:		280,000
Subsequent Years Costs:		128,000

MAINTENANCE:

Variable Initial Costs/Infrastructure:

Redtown hunting lodge:

Water system installation/hook-up:	3,000
Electrical hook-up:	5,000
Telephone hook-up:	1,000
Septic system hook-up:	8,000
Gravel/parking lot/roadways:	20,000
General repairs to building:	10,000

Compound construction/storage:	6,000
Residence:	
House/garage repairs:	15,000
Initial Year Costs:	68,000
Subsequent Years Cost:	15,000
TOTALS:	
Initial Year Costs:	348,000
Subsequent Years Costs:	143,000

Oversight. The Southwest Regional Office is located in Albuquerque, New Mexico, and provides oversight of refuge administration and management. The Regional Office also provides technical assistance on matters such as engineering, public use planning, and land acquisition services.

Facilities. The Service is responsible for maintaining facilities on its lands. Upon acquisition of any property, the Service will evaluate the condition and any need for retaining any structures or buildings. Structures or buildings may be kept for Service use, sold off for relocation to another site, sold for salvage or destroyed. If a structure is on, or eligible to be on, a state or national register of historic places, it can not be destroyed. It must be maintained or properly disposed of to an entity that will maintain it.

Roads. The Service is responsible for the management and maintenance of its own roads within refuge property. Public agencies retain the right to maintain any public roads that go through Service property.

Fencing and Signage. The Service is responsible for maintaining and signing its boundary fences and any public use facilities it develops. Any new fencing needed would also be the Service's responsibility.

IV.   Habitat Management

Refuge habitat management would focus on management of the mixed evergreen and deciduous bottomland forests and associated shrubby wetlands and marshes for wildlife management functions.

V.   Population Monitoring

Since the primary purpose for establishing a national wildlife refuge is wildlife conservation, surveys, are conducted yearly to track population trends. This information provides the basis for habitat management decisions and for monitoring their success. Surveys typically could include baseline vegetation surveys, stream fish surveys, herpetological surveys, migratory and breeding bird surveys, small mammal surveys, federally-listed threatened or endangered species surveys, and surface and groundwater quality monitoring. Once the refuge is expanded a schedule will be developed to do baseline inventory of plants, animals, etc. Academic research on refuge lands would be encouraged, as well as research by other agencies, because their findings provide additional information that assists with habitat management. The refuge will work with the Division of Planning, Remote Sensing Laboratory leading to the development of vegetation map and other data layers that will assist in the overall inventorying, monitoring, and adaptive management efforts.

VI. Public Use Opportunities and Management

National Wildlife Refuge System Priority Recreational Uses. The National Wildlife Refuge System Improvement Act of 1997 ensures that six priority wildlife-dependent recreational uses are strongly considered for integration into refuge programs provided they are determined compatible with the purposes for which the refuge was established and the Mission of the National Wildlife Refuge System as defined earlier. These six priority wildlife-dependent uses are:

> "... hunting, fishing, wildlife observation and photography, and environmental education, and interpretation."

The Act also insures that, on lands added to the Refuge System, existing compatible wildlife-dependent recreational uses will continue, pending completion of a comprehensive conservation plan (CCP) for the refuge. The Act ensures that the public is given an opportunity to participate in the process that determines whether an activity is compatible. Additionally, any management recommendations to discontinue uses found not to be compatible would most likely undergo National Environmental Policy Act (NEPA) compliance wherein the public is again given the opportunity to participate. If an existing use is legal, compatible, safe, consistent with sound fish and wildlife management principles, and otherwise in the public interest, the Service assesses whether it has the funding and staffing to administer that program. If those resources are insufficient, the new law requires the Service to seek out partners to assist in implementing that program. (For example, assistance from state conservation officers on a refuge in another state enabled that understaffed refuge to have at least a limited hunting program). Only after exhausting all possibilities for assistance from partners, can the Service prohibit an otherwise compatible, safe and sound wildlife-dependent public recreational use.

Therefore, the Service must determine the compatibility of recreational uses that are possible and contemplated to be part of a new or expanded refuge. Based upon the requirements of law, a draft determination is made available to the public for review prior to the final determination that is made. In the case of a new or expanded refuge, an "Interim" Compatibility is drafted (See Appendix 4: Interim Compatibility Determinations [draft])

VII. Development of a Comprehensive Conservation Plan

Within 10 years of establishment, the Refuge will develop a Comprehensive Conservation Plan (CCP) in accordance with the requirements of the National Wildlife Refuge System Improvement Act of 1997. The CCP will review any interim plans that were developed and establish a long term management proposal that will include the establishment of long term management goals, objectives, and strategies. These will include habitat management, recreational use management (i.e. hunting, fishing, wildlife observation, wildlife photography, and education), water management, fire management and a program for inventorying, and monitoring habitat and to some degree wildlife populations.

Appendix 1: References

Dallas Morning News. Texas Almanac, 2004-2005, edited by Elizabeth Cruce Alvarez, Texas A&M University Press Consortium, 672 pp.

Texas Committee on Natural Resources. 2003. Neches River Protection Initiative

Texas Historical Commission web site: http://www.thc.state.tx.us

Texas Parks and Wildlife Department. 2004. "The State of Rivers" in Texas Parks and Wildlife, the outdoor magazine of Texas, July 2004

Texas Water Development Board. 2002. Water for Texas.

U.S. Environmental Protection Agency Window to my Environment web site: http://www.epa.gov/enviro/wme/

U.S. Fish and Wildlife Service. 1979. Classification of Wetlands and Deepwater Habitats of the United States. By Lewis M. Cowardin, Virginia Carter, Francis C. Golet, and Edward T. LaRoe. Biological Services Program. FWS/OBS79/31.

U.S. Fish and Wildlife Service.1985a. Texas Bottomland Hardwood Preservation Program: Category 3. Division of Realty, Albuquerque, New Mexico.

U. S. Fish and Wildlife Service Biological Report 87(12), Synopsis of Wetland Functions and Values: Bottomland Hardwoods with Special Emphasis on Eastern Texas and Oklahoma. by D.L. Wilkinson, K. Schneller-McDonald, R.W. Olson, and G.T. Auble, 1987.

Appendix 2: Maps

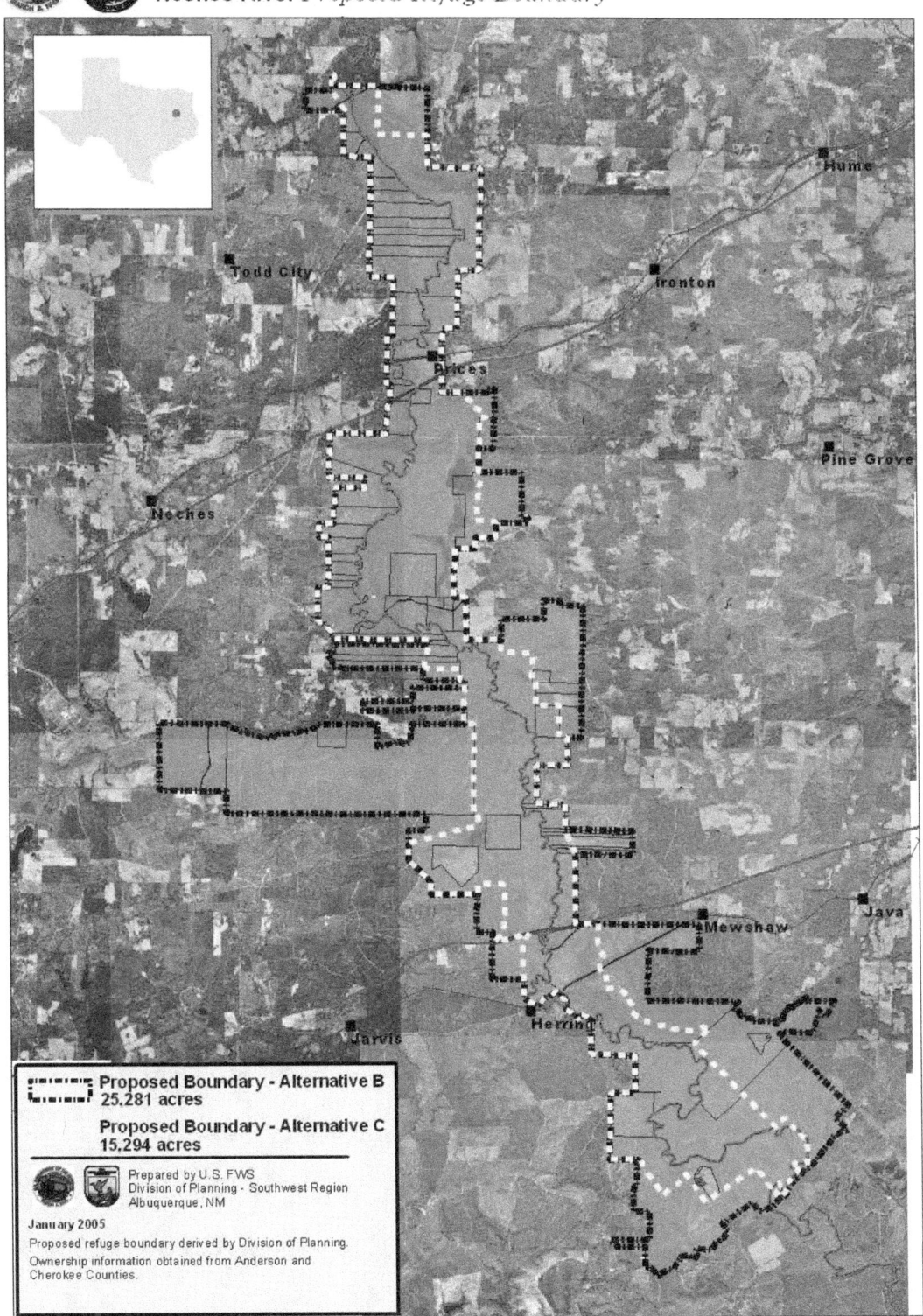

Hume

Todd City

Ironton

Prices

Pine Grove

Neches

Java

Mewshaw

Jarvis

Herring

Proposed Boundary - Alternative B
25,281 acres

Proposed Boundary - Alternative C
15,294 acres

Prepared by U.S. FWS
Division of Planning - Southwest Region
Albuquerque, NM

January 2005

Proposed refuge boundary derived by Division of Planning.
Ownership information obtained from Anderson and
Cherokee Counties.

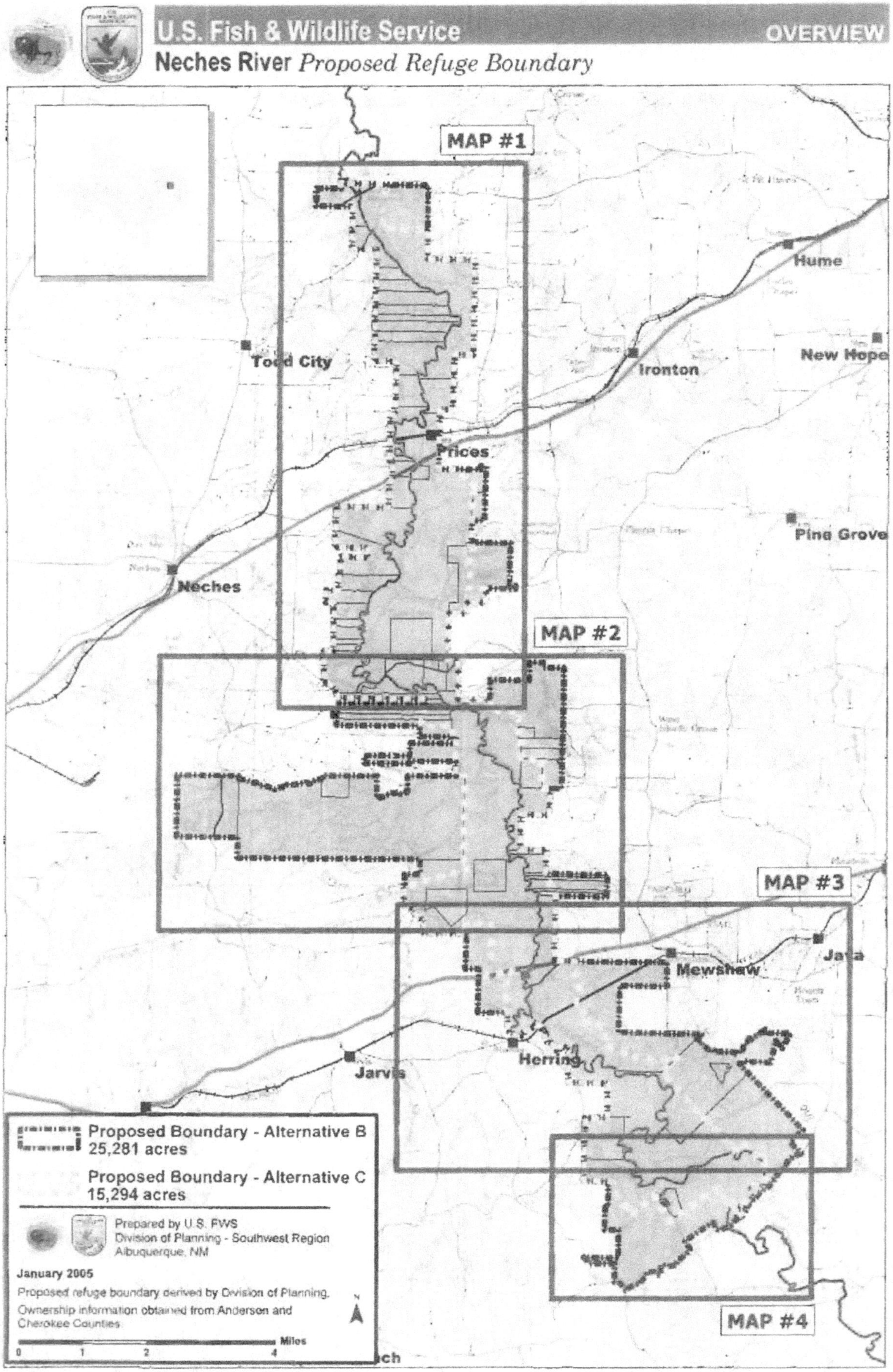

MAP #1

Hume

Todd City

Ironton

New Hope

Prices

Pina Grove

MAP #2

Neches

MAP #3

Mewshaw

Java

Herring

Jarvis

MAP #4

Proposed Boundary - Alternative B
25,281 acres

Proposed Boundary - Alternative C
15,294 acres

Prepared by U.S. FWS
Division of Planning - Southwest Region
Albuquerque, NM

January 2005

Proposed refuge boundary derived by Division of Planning.

Ownership information obtained from Anderson and
Cherokee Counties.

N

Miles
0   1   2   4

55

55

58

5

58

53

60

39

30

9

14

61

21

43

28

7

5

5

7

1

1 52

57

2

29

37

5

52

24

6

38

63

40

22

64

52

59

27

12 11 3

27

11 3

8

20

32

42 35

59

United States Highway

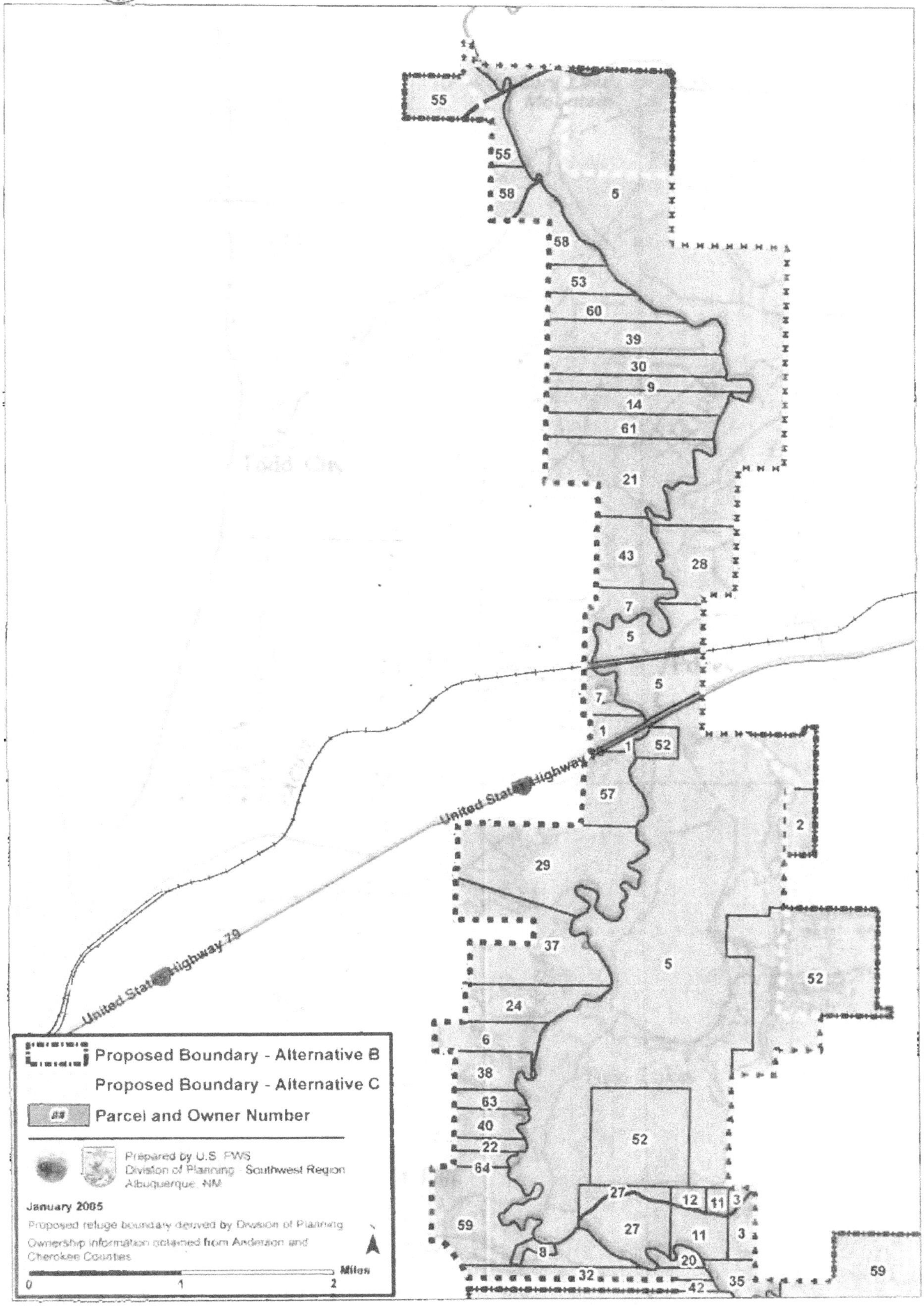

United States Highway 79

Proposed Boundary - Alternative B

Proposed Boundary - Alternative C

Parcel and Owner Number

Prepared by U.S. FWS
Division of Planning - Southwest Region
Albuquerque, NM

January 2005

Proposed refuge boundary derived by Division of Planning

Ownership information obtained from Anderson and
Cherokee Counties

Miles

0   1   2

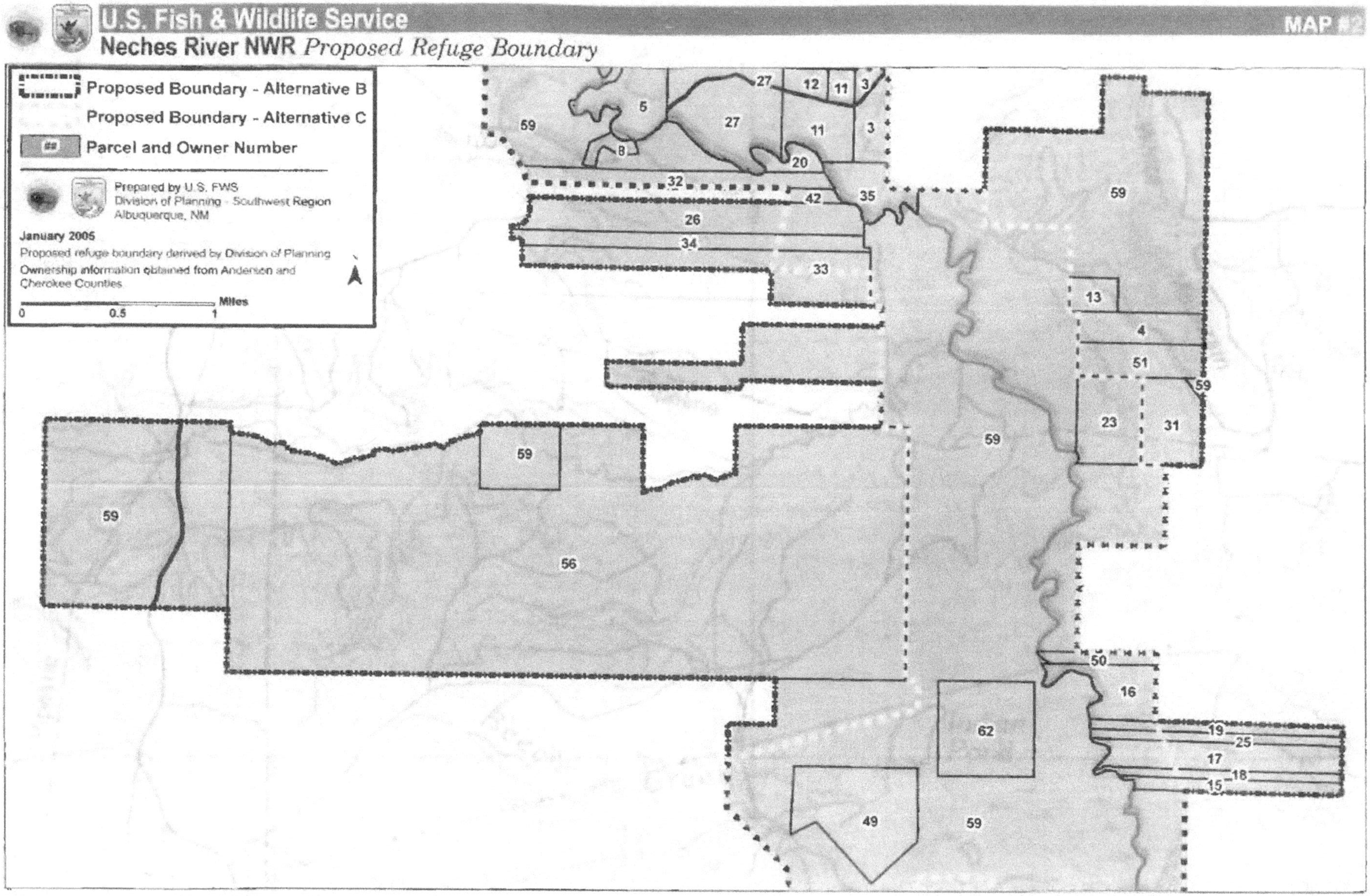

MAP 12

U.S. Fish & Wildlife Service

Neches River NWR *Proposed Refuge Boundary*

Proposed Boundary - Alternative B

Proposed Boundary - Alternative C

Parcel and Owner Number

##

Prepared by U.S. FWS
Division of Planning - Southwest Region
Albuquerque, NM

January 2005
Proposed refuge boundary derived by Division of Planning
Ownership information obtained from Anderson and
Cherokee Counties.

Miles

0   0.5   1

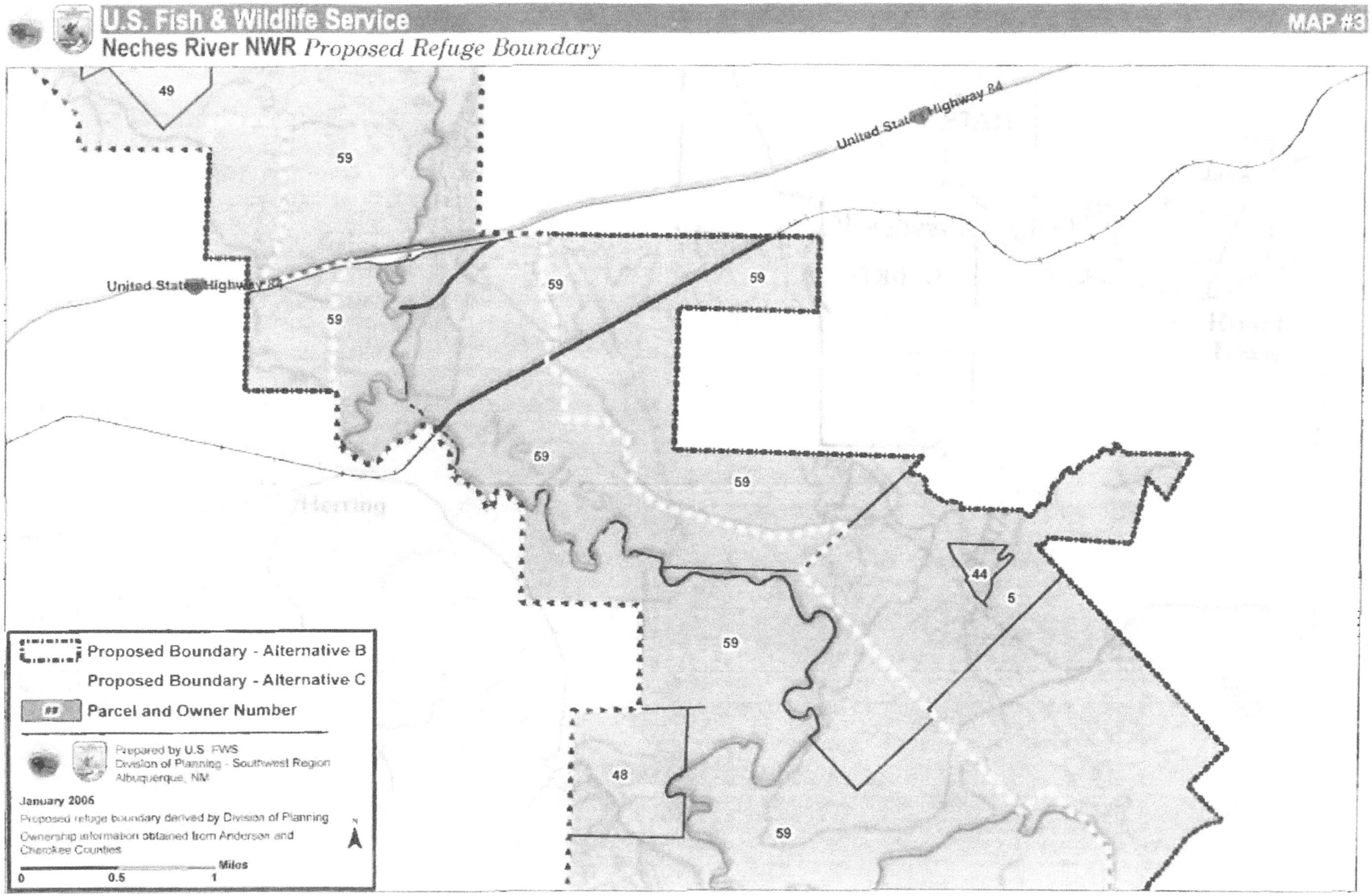

MAP #3

U.S. Fish & Wildlife Service

Neches River NWR *Proposed Refuge Boundary*

Highway 84

United States Highway 84

United States Highway 79

United States Highway 79

44

5

59

59

59

59

59

59

59

49

48

Neches River

Proposed Boundary - Alternative B

Proposed Boundary - Alternative C

Parcel and Owner Number

#

Prepared by U.S. FWS
Division of Planning - Southwest Region
Albuquerque, NM

January 2006

Proposed refuge boundary derived by Division of Planning

Ownership information obtained from Anderson and
Cherokee Counties

N

Miles

0   0.5   1

U.S. Fish & Wildlife Service
Neches River NWR *Proposed Refuge Boundary*

MAP

Proposed Boundary - Alternative B
Proposed Boundary - Alternative C

Parcel and Owner Number

Prepared by U.S. FWS
Division of Planning - Southwest Region
Albuquerque, NM

January 2005
Proposed refuge boundary derived by Division of Planning
Ownership information obtained from Anderson and
Cherokee Counties

Miles
0   0.5   1

Neches River NWR Proposed Boundary - Ownership List

Owner #	NAME	MAP #	DEEDED ACRES	PRIORITY	PROPERTY ID
1	ACORN RENTALS LLC	1	36.94	1	R25945
2	ALLETECH LABORATORIES	1	160.00	2	120008000
3	BATTON DANNY	1	60.41	1	116907011
4	BATTON FLORA R & BILLIE G	2	70.00	2	111762000
5	BLUE SKY TIMBER PRODUCTS LLC	1,3	300.00	2	100855000
5	BLUE SKY TIMBER PRODUCTS LLC	1,3	125.00	2	100856000
5	BLUE SKY TIMBER PRODUCTS LLC	1,3	60.00	2	100857000
5	BLUE SKY TIMBER PRODUCTS LLC	1,3	35.00	2	100858000
5	BLUE SKY TIMBER PRODUCTS LLC	1,3	48.00	2	100859000
5	BLUE SKY TIMBER PRODUCTS LLC	1,3	195.62	1	110068000
5	BLUE SKY TIMBER PRODUCTS LLC	1,3	780.95	1	112388000
5	BLUE SKY TIMBER PRODUCTS LLC	1,3	25.00	2	113425000
5	BLUE SKY TIMBER PRODUCTS LLC	1,3	170.00	1 & 2	114797000
5	BLUE SKY TIMBER PRODUCTS LLC	1,3	77.62	1	116238000
5	BLUE SKY TIMBER PRODUCTS LLC	1,3	317.45	2	119872000
5	BLUE SKY TIMBER PRODUCTS LLC	1,3	42.38	1	120396000
5	BLUE SKY TIMBER PRODUCTS LLC	1,3	159.37	1	120410000
5	BLUE SKY TIMBER PRODUCTS LLC	1,3	44.00	1	120475000
5	BLUE SKY TIMBER PRODUCTS LLC	1,3	73.48	1	120486000
6	BUCKLEY PENNY ETAL	1	39.48	1	R831434
6	BUCKLEY PENNY ETAL	1	1.11	1	R835329
7	CHENEY VICKIE L	1	20.85	1	R838218
8	CITY OF PALESTINE	1	22.63	1	R45660
9	CRIM MARGARET LANESSE	1	19.00	1	R20480
10	CROFT THOMAS S DR	4	22.70	1	R27623
10	CROFT THOMAS S DR	4	23.50	1	R27625
10	CROFT THOMAS S DR	4	11.70	1	R64869
11	DOLAN E P LIFE ESTATE	1	80.55	1	116907000
12	DOLAN MICHAEL J & ALLYCE K ETAL	1	20.14	1	116907010
13	DOWLING LUMBER CO INC	2	40.00	2	113554000
14	EATON GRACE T	1	62.54	1	R20484
15	EZELL D P	2	45.71	1 & 2	115240000
16	EZELL GLENN S & WANDA	2	60.17	1	115251000
17	EZELL PATRICK E	2	45.71	1 & 2	115241000
17	EZELL PATRICK E	2	45.71	1 & 2	115242000
17	EZELL PATRICK E	2	45.71	1 & 2	115245000
18	EZELL PHIL E &	2	45.71	1 & 2	115243000
19	EZELL R S	2	45.71	1 & 2	115244000
20	FIRST CITY TEXAS-TYLER N A TRUSTEE	1	24.70	1	R64835
21	FIVE DUCK HOLDINGS LLC	1	180.79	1	R20486
21	FIVE DUCK HOLDINGS LLC	1	69.08	1	R28100
22	FLETCHER-SCOTT TASHA	1	23.50	1	R21842
23	FLETCHER ROYCE	2	97.66	1	111763000
24	FLORCZAK HENRY	1	109.61	1	R21747
25	GEORGE FREDDIE C	2	45.71	1 & 2	115246000

26	HANDLEY STEVEN R ETUX CARRIE L	2	172.94	1 & 2	R833689
27	HOLMAN LUMAN & ROSEMARY	1	160.00	1	113699000
28	HOLSTEAD VALERIA S	1	20.29	1	110628000
29	HYPERION ENERGY L P	1	0.04	1	R45923
30	HYPERION RESOURCES INC	1	94.00	1	R20479
31	INGRAM MIKE SALES INC	2	89.22	2	111760000
32	JACKSON ALSIE VERNETTA	2	96.66	1	R20510
33	JACKSON LENA BELLE	2	16.12	1 & 2	R20523
33	JACKSON LENA BELLE	2	6.92	2	R20537
34	JACKSON PLEAS HEIRS	2	96.50	1 & 2	R20517
35	KENLEY DAVID C JR ESTATE	2	22.00	1	120477000
36	KUSEK LINDA L	4	0.97	1	R67946
37	LACY LINDBERGH M	1	143.00	1	R21745
37	LACY LINDBERGH M	1	125.00	1	R21913
38	LYLES JOHN EST	1	4.75	1	R21839
39	MARGRITZ RODNEY R & HARRY ADAMS	1	174.58	1	R20478
40	MATHIS F R ETAL	1	55.90	1	R21841
41	MCBROOM OZZIE GENELL	4	3.00	1	R64872
42	MILLER NANCY JACKSON ETAL	2	16.08	1	R20515
43	MULLINS RAYMOND & JANN FREEMAN	1	125.08	1	R28101
44	NEWMAN LIONEL	3	35.00	2	100845000
45	NIXON LEE ROY	4	1.46	1	R64871
46	PARKER CARLTON & CODY	4	0.97	1	R67947
47	PARKER EARL WAYNE	4	0.97	1	R27624
48	PEAVY JOHNNY JR	3	115.75	1	R27105
49	PETTY CAROLYN DUBLIN	2	183.52	1	R24891
50	POSEY RICHARD	2	30.08	1	115248000
51	RAINEY A C JR	2	70.00	2	111761000
52	RED TOWN TIMBER PRODUCTS, LP	1	33.70	1	111133000
52	RED TOWN TIMBER PRODUCTS, LP	1	46.50	1	112560000
52	RED TOWN TIMBER PRODUCTS, LP	1	28.20	1	113382000
52	RED TOWN TIMBER PRODUCTS, LP	1	281.00	1	113774000
52	RED TOWN TIMBER PRODUCTS, LP	1	320.00	1 & 2	119983000
53	RILEY HERBERT	1	64.04	1	R67470
54	ROBERTS JOYCELYN NIXON	4	1.46	1	R64870
55	RUSHING HENRY ETUX SHARON	1	130.79	1 & 2	R23121
55	RUSHING HENRY W ETUX SHARON A	1	28.48	1	R831938
56	SEALE DONALD	2	27.25	2	R830278
57	SMITH JAMES LEE	1	103.29	1	R61961
58	STATON JOE TIMBER PROPERTIES L P	1	130.18	1	R26359
59	TEMPLE-INLAND INC	1,2,3,4	652.00	2	100862000
59	TEMPLE-INLAND INC	1,2,3,4	318.40	2	100868000
59	TEMPLE-INLAND INC	1,2,3,4	120.00	2	110458000
59	TEMPLE-INLAND INC	1,2,3,4	39.72	2	110459000
59	TEMPLE-INLAND INC	1,2,3,4	320.00	1 & 2	111757000
59	TEMPLE-INLAND INC	1,2,3,4	311.33	2	113263000
59	TEMPLE-INLAND INC	1,2,3,4	302.30	1 & 2	113351000
59	TEMPLE-INLAND INC	1,2,3,4	280.00	2	113555000
59	TEMPLE-INLAND INC	1,2,3,4	249.00	1 & 2	113809000
59	TEMPLE-INLAND INC	1,2,3,4	161.54	1 & 2	114966000
59	TEMPLE-INLAND INC	1,2,3,4	640.00	1 & 2	116494000

59	TEMPLE-INLAND INC	1,2,3,4	41.20	1	120026000
59	TEMPLE-INLAND INC	1,2,3,4	1397.36	1	120081000
59	TEMPLE-INLAND INC	1,2,3,4	139.50	1	120215000
59	TEMPLE-INLAND INC	1,2,3,4	182.00	1	120289000
59	TEMPLE-INLAND INC	1,2,3,4	146.50	1	120474000
59	TEMPLE-INLAND INC	1,2,3,4	426.37	1	R19648
59	TEMPLE-INLAND INC	1,2,3,4	575.00	1 & 2	R20576
59	TEMPLE-INLAND INC	1,2,3,4	679.80	1	R21208
59	TEMPLE-INLAND INC	1,2,3,4	320.00	2	R21625
59	TEMPLE-INLAND INC	1,2,3,4	615.00	2	R21988
59	TEMPLE-INLAND INC	1,2,3,4	96.40	2	R23247
59	TEMPLE-INLAND INC	1,2,3,4	319.18	1 & 2	R24889
59	TEMPLE-INLAND INC	1,2,3,4	434.60	1 & 2	R24890
59	TEMPLE-INLAND INC	1,2,3,4	160.00	1 & 2	R26444
59	TEMPLE-INLAND INC	1,2,3,4	117.27	1	R27109
59	TEMPLE-INLAND INC	1,2,3,4	75.50	1	R27626
59	TEMPLE-INLAND INC	1,2,3,4	1280.00	1 & 2	R27691
59	TEMPLE-INLAND INC	1,2,3,4	1168.67	2	R27722
59	TEMPLE-INLAND INC	1,2,3,4	314.63	1 & 2	R27865
59	TEMPLE-INLAND INC	1,2,3,4	476.59	1	R27882
59	TEMPLE-INLAND INC	1,2,3,4	166.10	1	R28048
59	TEMPLE-INLAND INC	1,2,3,4	101.00	1	R28103
59	TEMPLE-INLAND INC	1,2,3,4	456.00	1	R28170
59	TEMPLE-INLAND INC	1,2,3,4	5.23	2	111764000
59	TEMPLE-INLAND FOREST PRODUCTS	1,2,3,4	4086.25	1 & 2	R20647
60	THADEN MARION VIRGINIA	1	58.40	1	R26365
60	THADEN MARION VIRGINIA	1	14.60	1	R26366
61	WESTON ROYCE V ETUX JANET J	1	125.08	1	R20485
62	WOODS ARTHUR LEE ETUX BONITA	2	16.60	1	R21748
63	WORTHY JAMES EST	1	59.00	1	R21840
64	YOUNT ANNIE P	1	21.50	1	R21843

Appendix 3: Federal Laws and Regulations Applicable to Preservation and Management of Fish and Wildlife Resources

Antiquities Act of 1906 (34 Stat. 225). Provided for protection of artifacts and historical objects and their recovery by accredited institutions.

Bald and Golden Eagles Protection Act of 1940 (16 U.S.C. 668- 668d; 54 Stat. 250). Provides for protection of the bald eagle (the national emblem) and the golden eagle.

Criminal Code Provisions of 1940 (18 U.S.C. 41), as amended. States the intent of Congress to protect all wildlife within Federal sanctuaries, refuges, fish hatcheries, and breeding grounds, and provides that anyone except in compliance with rules and regulations promulgated by authority of law, who hunts, traps, or willfully disturbs any such wildlife, or willfully injures, molests, or destroys any property of the United States on such land or water shall be fined up to $500.00 or imprisoned for not more than six (6) months or both.

Emergency Wetland Resources Act of 1986. Provides for 1) an extension of Wetlands Loan Act until September 30, 1988; 2) sale of admission permits at certain National Wildlife Refuges; 3) increasing the price of the Migratory Bird Hunting and Conservation Stamp to $10.00 in hunting years 1987 and 1988, $12.50 for hunting years 1989 and 1990, and $15.00 for each hunting year thereafter; 4) transfers import duties collected on arms and ammunition to Migratory Bird Conservation Fund ; 5) establishment of National Wetlands Priority Conservation Plan; 6) use of Land and Water Conservation Fund monies for acquisition of wetlands for migratory birds; 7) inclusion of wetlands in statewide outdoor recreation plans; 8) acquisition of wetlands; 9) certain restrictions on use of eminent domain in wetland acquisition; and 10) continuation of National Wetlands Inventory Project.

Endangered Species Act of 1973 (16 U.S.C. 1531, et seq.; 87 Stat. 884). This Act provides for the conservation of threatened and endangered species of fish, wildlife, and plants by Federal action and by encouraging State programs. Specific provisions include: (1) authorizes the listing and determination of critical habitat of endangered or threatened species and requires consultation with the Service on any federally funded or licensed project that could affect any of these species or their habitat; (2) prohibits unauthorized taking, possession, sale, transport, etc. of endangered species; (3) authorizes an expanded program of habitat acquisition; (4) authorizes the establishment of cooperative agreements and grant-in-aid to States which establish and maintain an active, adequate program for endangered and threatened species; and (5) authorizes the assessment of civil and criminal penalties for violating the Act or regulations.

Fish and Wildlife Act of 1956 (16 U.S.C. 742a-742j; 70 Stat. 1119). Approved August 8, 1956, the Act established a comprehensive fish and wildlife policy and directed the Secretary to provide continuing research, extension and information services; and directed development, management, and conservation of fish and wildlife resources.

Food Security Act (Farm Bill) of 1990 as amended (HR2100) The provisions of the 1990 farm bill makes the goals of the U.S. Department of Agriculture farm and conservation programs more consistent. The conservation reserve, conservation compliance, and sodbuster and swamp buster provisions of the bill encourage reduction of soil erosion, retention of wetlands, and reduction protection of surplus commodities

Land and Water Conservation Fund Act of 1965. This Act provides financial assistance to the States for outdoor recreation, primarily in (1) planning; (2) acquisition of land, water, or interests in land or waters; or (3) development.

In addition to assistance to the States, the Land and Water Conservation Fund Act provides that not less than 40 percent of the annual appropriation shall be available for Federal purposes. Funds appropriated for Federal purposes shall be made available for the acquisition of land, waters, or interests in land or waters for the (1) National Park System, (2) National Forest System, (3) National Wildlife Refuge System, and (4) Bureau of Land Management.

The appropriations provided by Land and Water Conservation Fund Act are derived from Outer Continental Shelf leases, tax on motorboat fuels, and sale of certain surplus Federal lands. The Act also increased Land and Water Conservation Fund authorization for FY 1978 and the following years through FY 1989.

The Fish and Wildlife Service utilizes four basic acquisition authorities which are allowed through the funding authority of Land and Water Conservation Fund Act to purchase land and water, including (1) Endangered Species Act of 1973; (2) Refuge Recreation Act of 1962; (3) Fish and Wildlife Act of 1956, except for migratory waterfowl areas; and (4) any areas authorized as additions to the National Wildlife Refuge System by specific Congressional Acts.

Migratory Bird Treaty Act of 1918 (16 U.S.C. 703-711; 40 Stat. 755). Implements treaties with Great Britain (for Canada), Mexico, Japan, and Soviet Union for protection of migratory birds whose welfare is a Federal responsibility; provides for regulations to control taking, possessing, selling, transporting, and importing of migratory birds and provides penalties for violations.

Migratory Bird Conservation Act of 1929 (16 U.S.C. 715-715r; 45 Stat. 1222). Authorizes acquisition, development, and maintenance of migratory, bird refuges; cooperation with other agencies in conservation; and investigations and publications on North American Birds.

Migratory Bird Hunting Stamp Act 1934 (16 U.S.C. 718 - 718h; 48 Stat. 451). Requires that all waterfowl hunters, sixteen (16) years of age or older possess a valid "duck stamp"; required use of "duck stamp" net revenue to acquire migratory bird refuges and waterfowl production areas.

The National Environmental Policy Act of 1969, NEPA (42 U.S.C. 4321, et seq.; 83 Stat. 852). Declares the national policy to encourage a productive and enjoyable harmony between man and his environment. Section 102 of that Act directs that "to the fullest extent possible: (1) the policies, regulations, and public laws of the United States shall be interpreted and administered in accordance with the policies set forth in this Act, and (2) all agencies of the Federal Government shall ... insure that presently unquantified environmental amenities and values may be given appropriate consideration in decision making along with economic and technical considerations. . . "

Section 102 (2)c of the National Environmental Policy Act requires all Federal Agencies, with respect to major Federal actions significantly affecting the quality of the human environment, prepare a detailed statement on:

(i)   The environmental impact of the proposed action;
(ii) Any adverse environmental effect which cannot be avoided should the proposal be implemented;
(iii) Alternatives to the proposed action;
(iv) The relationship between local short-term uses of man's environment and the maintenance and enhancement of long-term productivity;
(v)   Any irreversible and irretrievable commitments of resources which would be involved in the proposed action should it be implemented.

National Historic Preservation Act of 1966 (16 U.S.C. 470, et seq.; 80 Stat. 915). The Act provides for the preservation of significant historical features (buildings, objects, etc.) through a grant-in-aid program to the States. Establishes a National Register of Historic Places. Federal Agencies are required to consider the effects of their actions on buildings, etc., included or eligible for inclusion in the National Register.

National Wildlife Refuge System Administration Act of 1966 (16 U.S.C. 668dd, 668ee; 80 Stat. 927). Consolidates the authorities for the various categories of areas previously established that are administered by the Secretary of the Interior for the conservation of fish and wildlife, including species that are threatened with extinction. All lands, waters, and interests therein administered by the Secretary as wildlife refuges, etc., are hereby designated as the National Wildlife Refuge System. Provides, according to the Act, that the Secretary may authorize hunting and fishing to the extent practicable and consistent with State fish and wildlife laws and regulations.

National Wildlife Refuge System Improvement Act of 1997 (Public Law 105-57) This Act provides clarification of the mission of the National Wildlife Refuge System and general management principles for the more than 500 refuges in the system. It identifies six priority public uses that are wildlife dependent that require consideration in the management of refuges: hunting, fishing, wildlife observation, photography, interpretation and environmental education. All other proposed public uses must be examined for their compatibility with the purposes for which each refuge is established.

National Wildlife Refuge Regulations for the most recent fiscal year (50 CFR Subchapter C; 43 CFR 3101.3-3). Provides regulations for administration and management of wildlife refuge areas including mineral leasing, exploration, and development.

North American Wetlands Conservation Act of 1990. Encourage partnership among public agencies and other interests to: (1) protect, restore, and manage an appropriate distribution and diversity of wetland ecosystems and other habitats for migratory birds and other fish and wildlife; (2) maintain distribution of migratory bird populations; and

(3) sustain an abundance of waterfowl and other migratory birds consistent with the goals of the North American Waterfowl Management Plan.

Appropriations provided by the North American Wetlands Conservation Act are derived from Federal Aid in Wildlife Restoration Act (Pittman-Robertson) funds and proceeds from migratory bird fines, penalties, and forfeitures under the Migratory Bird Treaty Act. Appropriations are not to exceed $15 million beginning in FY 1991 and continuing through 1994. Allocation of funding from the Act provides at least 50 percent, but not more than 70 percent of available funds for projects in Canada and Mexico. At least 30 percent, but not more than 50 percent of available funds will be appropriated for projects in the United States.

Refuge Recreation Act of 1962 (16 U.S.C. 460k-460k-4; 76 Stat. 653). Authorizes appropriate, incidental, or secondary recreational use on conservation area administered by the Secretary of the Interior for fish and wildlife purposes.

Refuge Revenue Sharing Act of 1935, as amended in 1978, (16 U.S.C. 715s; 92 Stat. 1319). Makes revenue sharing applicable to all lands solely or primarily administered by the Service, whereas previously it was applicable only to areas in the National Wildlife Refuge System. The new law makes payments available for any governmental purpose, whereas the old law restricted the use of payments to roads and schools. For fee (acquired) lands, the new law provides a payment of 75 cents per acre, ¾ of 1 percent of fair market value, or 25 percent of net receipts, whichever is greater, whereas the old law provided a payment of ¾ of 1 percent adjusted cost or 25 percent of net receipts, whichever was greater. For reserve (public domain) lands, the law provides for a payment of 25 percent of net receipts. The new law authorizes appropriations to make up any short-fall in net receipts to make payments in the full amount for which counties are eligible. The old law provided that if the net receipts were insufficient to make the full payment, the payment to each county would be reduced proportionately.

Refuge Trespass Act of June 25, 1948 (18 U.S.C. 41; 62 Stat. 686). The Act makes it unlawful to hunt, trap, capture, willfully disturb, or kill any bird or wild animal, or take or destroy the eggs of any such birds on any lands of the United States set apart or reserved as refuges or breeding grounds for such birds or animals by any law, proclamation, or executive order, except under rules and regulations of the Secretary. The Act also protects Government property on such lands.

Wilderness Act (16 U.S.C. 1131; 78 Stat. 890). Establishes the wilderness system as a supplement to the purposes for which units of the National Wildlife Refuge System are established.

Use of Off-Road Vehicles on Public Lands (Executive Order 11644, as amended by Executive Order 11989). Provides policy and procedures for regulating off-road vehicles.

Appendix 4: ANSWERS TO FREQUENTLY ASKED QUESTIONS ABOUT SELLING LAND TO THE U.S. FISH AND WILDLIFE SERVICE

What if I don't want to sell my land?

You don't have to. The Service buys from willing sellers only. You can continue to use your land as you like and sell it to anyone you like.

How is the sale price determined?

An experienced and qualified appraiser who is familiar with the area will conduct a market-based appraisal comparing your property with recently completed sales of similar properties in the market area. All appraisals must be prepared in an unbiased and professional manner in accordance with the Uniform Appraisal Standards for Federal Land Acquisitions to determine fair market value. If your property is worth over $1,000,000, two appraisals will be completed by different appraisers. All appraisals are reviewed and approved by an Interior Department review appraiser, who has had many years of appraisal experience. A federal law, The Uniform Relocation Assistance and Real Property Acquisition Policies Act requires that landowners be invited to accompany the appraiser on their land; that only fair market offers be made; and that the federal agency reimburse businesses, farms, homeowners and tenants for relocation expenses.

How long will it take to sell or donate my land?

The Service needs time to comply with the National Environmental Policy Act and other laws before any land can be purchased. Funding must be available to purchase lands. Generally, from initial meeting to closing can take from 4 months to a year, depending on the quality of the title, the number of joint owners, the complexity of reservations or exceptions, the size of the tract and kind of improvements, and the complexity of any businesses or leases on the property. Occasionally, special circumstances may stretch the process out longer, such as difficulties in coming to joint owner agreements or bad weather hampering access for appraisers.

Do I need a real estate agent?

We can work directly with the landowner. We are required by law to present the approved appraised value to the landowner in the form of a Statement of Just Compensation; this constitutes our offer to the landowner. You may use an agent, however, the agreement is between you and the agent. The Service does not pay brokerage fees or fees charged by attorneys retained by the landowner. The appraiser is also required to contact the landowner, as mentioned above. If you do use an agent, the appraiser would like a copy of the written assignment so the agent can also be contacted.

What happens after I sign a purchase agreement?

The Service will accept the purchase agreement and send a letter of acceptance to the landowner. Concurrently, a title package, that includes a signed purchase agreement and title commitment, is submitted to the Department of Interior's Field Solicitor (attorney) for his review of the title condition to satisfy the requirements of Department of Justice Standards. If the condition of title is satisfactory, the Solicitor issues an opinion that gives the Service the authority to order the payment for the purchase of the land and to close on the property. A closing is arranged with a closing agent at the title company.

Who pays for closing costs?

The Service pays for the closing fees. See the brochure titled "A Legacy for the Future," for information on other expenses paid by the Service that are incidental to the transfer of title. The Service does not pay for expenses associated with perfecting the title on the land.

Who pays for property taxes?

The landowner is responsible for payment of the taxes up to the date of title transfer. The closing agent will arrange with the county taxing agency for the proration of taxes to the date of transfer. All prior year taxes should be paid by the landowner.

Can I sell or donate my land and continue to live on it?

The Service often grants a life use, especially to older residents, enabling them to continue living on the property for the remainder of their life, or until they move. Their home and immediate outbuildings and animal pens, remain under the resident's control. The resident no longer pays taxes, but must keep insurance on the home. The sale price may be reduced depending on a formula that takes into account the resident's age and standard life expectancy rates.

What other options do I have if I do not want to sell in fee simple?

You can convey a conservation easement. In this case, the Service would purchase a non-development interest in the land, but the fee title remains with the landowner, and landowner would continue to pay taxes on the property. The landowner would agree to maintain the land in an undeveloped state or in a state existing at the time of purchase in accordance with terms that would be specified in the easement. The acquisition of easements generally follow the same procedure as for purchase of fee title, that is, an appraisal will be made to determine the fair market value of the interest to be purchased.

Where does the money to buy land come from?

The Migratory Bird Conservation Fund comes mainly from revenues from the sale of Federal Waterfowl Hunting Stamps ("duck stamps"). The Migratory Bird Conservation Commission in Washington D.C. must approve the purchase of new tracts for migratory bird refuges.

Can I keep my mineral interest if I sell my surface interest?

You may keep your mineral interest. The refuge manager works with drilling operators on a cooperative basis to minimize any adverse environmental effects. The Service also respects third party mineral interests.

Can I pursue a sale or donation of my land to a non-profit organization for habitat conservation purposes?

There are several organizations that acquire lands for conservation purposes including The Conservation Fund, The Nature Conservancy, Trust for Public Lands, and, where they exist, local land trusts. These organizations are often able to provide innovative estate, income and tax benefit options for land.

Appendix 5:   Pre acquisition Interim Compatibility
               Determinations (draft)

DRAFT INTERIM COMPATIBILITY DETERMINATION

Use: Wildlife Observation

Refuge Name: Neches River National Wildlife Refuge

Establishing and Acquisition Authorities: The Migratory Bird Conservation Act of 1929, as, amended, the Fish and Wildlife Act of 1956 and the Land and Water Conservation Fund Act of 1963, as amended.

Refuge Purposes: The purposes for the refuge will be:

- ... For the development, advancement, management, conservation, and protection of fish and wildlife resources ... 16 U.S.C. 742(b)(1)(Fish and Wildlife Act of 1956).
- ... For use as an inviolate sanctuary, or for any other management purpose, for migratory birds. 16 U.S.C. 715d (Migratory Bird Conservation Act)
- ... For the conservation of...wetlands...and to help fulfill international obligations contained in various migratory bird treaties and conventions. 16 U.S.C. 3901(b)

The refuge will be established to fulfill the above purposes by:

- Protecting, restoring, and maintaining the bottomland hardwood forest plant community,
- Protecting and enhancing habitat for migratory bird use, and
- Protecting and enhancing habitat to sustain healthy populations of native fish and wildlife species.

This will be accomplished through an ecosystem approach that protects the bottomland hardwood habitat resources and the diversity of wildlife therein.

National Wildlife Refuge System Mission: To administer a national network of lands and waters for the conservation, management, and where appropriate, restoration of the fish, wildlife, and plant resources and their habitats within the United States for the benefit of present and future generations of Americans.

Description of Use: Wildlife Observation

This use is either the ultimate public use goal of visitors or it is incidental to some other use or activity.

Availability of Resources: Most of the refuge's units will be in remote rural, bottomland hardwood forested areas. At this time most parking facilities are limited to a few automobiles on dirt trails. In the short term, the refuge will be managed as a satellite of the Little River National Wildlife Refuge Complex in Broken Bow, Oklahoma. Neches River National Wildlife Refuge's staff will consists of a manager who is stationed at Caddo Lake National Wildlife Refuge and will be assisted by personnel from the Little River National Wildlife Refuge for biological, clerical, law enforcement, and maintenance support.

Anticipated Impacts of the Use: If there is any question that a public use may harm Service trust species, the refuge manager should always decide for wildlife protection over public use. Wildlife observation practiced on migratory bird habitats may have only temporary or negligible effects on Service trust resources.

Public Review and Comment: This compatibility determination will be circulated for public review and comment with the Conceptual Management Plan, the Environmental Assessment, and Land Protection Plan for the proposed refuge establishment for 45 days in 2005. The National Wildlife Refuge System Improvement Act of 1997 ensures that wildlife photography, one of the six priority wildlife-dependent recreational uses, is considered for integration into refuge programs if determined to be compatible with the purposes for which the refuge is established. The Act ensures that lands added to the refuge System with existing compatible wildlife-dependent recreational uses will continue, pending completion of a Comprehensive Conservation Plan for the refuge. With appropriate management, the activity of wildlife photography should not affect accomplishment of the refuge purposes. Depending upon seasonal considerations, there may be parts of the refuge lands that will be periodically off limits to recreational uses. At times, such activities may be subject to the issuance of a permit. The Act insures that the public is given an opportunity to participate in the process that determines whether or not an activity is compatible.

Determination (check one below):

_____ **Use is Not Compatible**

_X_ **Use is Compatible With Following Stipulations**

Stipulations Necessary to Ensure Compatibility:

Public or legal access to tracts must be available.

Vehicle and/or all-terrain vehicle use may be restricted to prevent damage to refuge resources.

Some areas may be subject to seasonal closures during migratory bird use periods.

Justification: The Service believes one of the key needs of our society is environmental education leading to an appreciation and advocacy of our natural resources. This is also a key goal for the Neches River National Wildlife Refuge as well.

Signatures: **Refuge Manager:**

_____

                                    (Signature and Date)

Concurrence: Regional Chief:

_____

                                    (Signature and Date)

Mandatory 10- or 15-year Re-evaluation Date:

_____2015_____

DRAFT INTERIM COMPATIBILITY DETERMINATION

Use: Wildlife Photography

Refuge Name: Neches River National Wildlife Refuge

Establishing and Acquisition Authorities: The Migratory Bird Conservation Act of 1929, as, amended, the Fish and Wildlife Act of 1956 and the Land and Water Conservation Fund Act of 1963, as amended.

Refuge Purposes: The purposes for the refuge will be:

- ... For the development, advancement, management, conservation, and protection of fish and wildlife resources ...16 U.S.C. 742(b)(1)(Fish and Wildlife Act of 1956).

- ... For use as an inviolate sanctuary, or for any other management purpose, for migratory birds. 16 U.S.C. 715d (Migratory Bird Conservation Act)

- ... For the conservation of...wetlands...and to help fulfill international obligations contained in various migratory bird treaties and conventions. 16 U.S.C. ○ 3901(b)

The refuge will be established to achieve the above listed refuge purposes by:
- Protecting, restoring, and maintaining the bottomland hardwood forest plant community,
- Protecting and enhancing habitat for migratory bird use, and
- Protecting and enhancing habitat to sustain healthy populations of native fish and wildlife species.

This will be accomplished through an ecosystem approach that protects the bottomland hardwood habitat resources and the diversity of wildlife they support.

National Wildlife Refuge System Mission: To administer a national network of lands and waters for the conservation, management, and where appropriate, restoration of the fish, wildlife, and plant resources and their habitats within the United States for the benefit of present and future generations of Americans.

Description of Use: Wildlife photography

This use is either the ultimate public use goal of visitors or it is incidental to some other use or activity, primarily wildlife observation. Recreational objectives will provide opportunities for wildlife photography.

Availability of Resources: Most of the refuge's units will be in remote rural, bottomland hardwood forested areas. At this time most parking facilities are limited to a few automobiles on dirt trails. In the short term, the refuge will be managed as a satellite of the Little River National Wildlife Refuge Complex in Broken Bow, Oklahoma. Neches River National Wildlife Refuge's staff will consist of a manager who is stationed at Caddo Lake National Wildlife Refuge who will be assisted by personnel from the Little River National Wildlife Refuge for biological, clerical, law enforcement, and maintenance support.

Anticipated Impacts of the Use: If there is any question that a public use may harm Service trust species, the refuge manager should always decide for wildlife protection over public use. Wildlife photography practiced on migratory bird habitats may have only temporary or negligible effects on Service trust resources.

Public Review and Comment: This compatibility determination will be circulated for public review and comment with the Conceptual Management Plan, the Environmental Assessment, and Land Protection Plan for the proposed refuge establishment for 45 days in 2005. The National Wildlife Refuge System Improvement Act of 1997 ensures wildlife photography, one of the six priority wildlife-dependent recreational uses, is considered for integration into refuge programs provided it is determined compatible with the purposes for which the refuge was established. The Act insures that lands added to the refuge System with existing compatible wildlife-dependent recreational uses will continue, pending completion of a comprehensive conservation plan for the refuge. With appropriate management, future use for wildlife photography should not affect accomplishment of the refuge purposes. The Act insures that the public is given an opportunity to participate in the process that determines whether or not an activity is compatible.

Determination (check one below):

_____ **Use is not compatible**

_X_ **Use is Compatible with Following Stipulations**

Stipulations Necessary to Ensure Compatibility:

Public or legal access to tracts must be available.

Vehicle and/or all-terrain vehicle use may be restricted to prevent damage to refuge resources.

Some areas may be subject to seasonal closure during migratory bird use periods.

Justification: The Service believes one of the key needs of our society is wildlife photography leading to an appreciation and advocacy of our natural resources. This is also a key goal for the Neches River National Wildlife Refuge as well.

Signatures: **Refuge Manager:** _____

(Signature and Date)

Concurrence: Regional Chief: _____

(Signature and Date)

Mandatory 10- or 15-year Re-evaluation Date: _____2015_____

DRAFT INTERIM COMPATIBILITY DETERMINATION

Use: Interpretation

Refuge Name: Neches River National Wildlife Refuge

Establishing and Acquisition Authorities: The Migratory Bird Conservation Act of 1929, as, amended, the Fish and Wildlife Act of 1956 and the Land and Water Conservation Fund Act of 1963, as amended.

Refuge Purposes: The purposes for the refuge will be:

- ... For the development, advancement, management, conservation, and protection of fish and wildlife resources ...16 U.S.C. 742(b)(1)(Fish and Wildlife Act of 1956).

- ... For use as an inviolate sanctuary, or for any other management purpose, for migratory birds. 16 U.S.C. 715d (Migratory Bird Conservation Act)

- .. For the conservation of...wetlands...and to help fulfill international obligations contained in various migratory bird treaties and conventions. 16 U.S.C. ○ 3901(b)

The refuge will be established to achieve the above listed refuge purposes by:
- Protecting, restoring, and maintaining the bottomland hardwood forest plant community,
- Protecting and enhancing habitat for migratory bird use, and
- Protecting and enhancing habitat to sustain healthy populations of native fish and wildlife species.

This will be accomplished through an ecosystem approach that protects the bottomland hardwood plant community and wildlife resources.

National Wildlife Refuge System Mission: To administer a national network of lands and waters for the conservation, management, and where appropriate, restoration of the fish, wildlife, and plant resources and their habitats within the United States for the benefit of present and future generations of Americans.

Description of Use: Interpretation

This use typically involves persons or groups of varying ages observing on-site presentations by expert guides about the biological or ecological topics regarding the site.

Availability of Resources: Most of the refuge's units will be in remote rural, bottomland hardwood forested areas. At this time most parking facilities are limited to a few automobiles on dirt trails. The refuge currently is managed as a satellite of the Little River National Wildlife Refuge Complex in Broken Bow, Oklahoma. Neches River National Wildlife Refuge's staff will consists of a manager who is stationed at Caddo Lake National Wildlife Refuge and will be assisted by personnel from the Little River National Wildlife Refuge for biological, clerical, law enforcement, and maintenance support.

Anticipated Impacts of the Use: If there is any question that a public use may harm Service trust species, the refuge manager should always decide for wildlife protection over public use. Interpretation practiced on migratory bird habitats may have only temporary or negligible effects on Service trust resources.

Public Review and Comment: This compatibility determination will be circulated for public review and comment with the Draft Conceptual Management Plan, the Environmental Assessment, and Land Protection Plan for the proposed refuge establishment for 45 days in 2005. The National Wildlife Refuge System Improvement Act of 1997 ensures wildlife photography, one of the six priority wildlife-dependent recreational uses, is considered for integration into refuge programs provided it is determined compatible with the purposes for which the refuge was established. The Act insures that lands added to the refuge System with existing compatible wildlife-dependent recreational uses will continue, pending completion of a comprehensive conservation plan for the refuge. With appropriate management, future use for wildlife photography should not affect accomplishment of the refuge purposes. The Act insures that the public is given an opportunity to participate in the process that determines whether or not an activity is compatible.

Determination (check one below):

_____ **Use is not compatible**

_X_ **Use is Compatible with Following Stipulations**

Stipulations Necessary to Ensure Compatibility:

Public or legal access to tracts must be available.

Vehicle and/or all-terrain vehicle use may be restricted to prevent damage to refuge resources.

Some areas may be subject to seasonal closures during migratory bird use periods.

Justification: The Service believes one of the key needs of our society is environmental education leading to an appreciation and advocacy of our natural resources. This is also a key goal for the Neches River National Wildlife Refuge as well.

Signatures: **Refuge Manager:** _____

(Signature and Date)

Concurrence: Regional Chief: _____

(Signature and Date)

Mandatory 10- or 15-year Re-evaluation Date: _____2015_____

DRAFT INTERIM COMPATIBILITY DETERMINATION

Use: Recreational Fishing

Refuge Name: Neches River National Wildlife Refuge

Establishing and Acquisition Authorities: The Migratory Bird Conservation Act of 1929, as, amended, the Fish and Wildlife Act of 1956 and the Land and Water Conservation Fund Act of 1963, as amended.

Refuge Purposes: The purposes for the refuge will be:

- ... For the development, advancement, management, conservation, and protection of fish and wildlife resources ...16 U.S.C. 742(b)(1)(Fish and Wildlife Act of 1956).
- ... For use as an inviolate sanctuary, or for any other management purpose, for migratory birds. 16 U.S.C. 715d (Migratory Bird Conservation Act)
- ... For the conservation of...wetlands...and to help fulfill international obligations contained in various migratory bird treaties and conventions. 16 U.S.C. 3901(b)

The refuge will be established to achieve the above listed purposes by:
Protecting, restoring, and maintaining the bottomland hardwood forest biotic community,
Protecting and enhancing habitat for migratory bird use, and
Protecting and enhancing habitats to sustain healthy populations of native fish and wildlife species.

National Wildlife Refuge System Mission: To administer a national network of lands and waters for the conservation, management, and where appropriate, restoration of the fish, wildlife, and plant resources and their habitats within the United States for the benefit of present and future generations of Americans.

Description of Use: Recreational Fishing

If areas are acquired that provide fishing opportunities and do not conflict with refuge management objectives, the Service will make every effort to provide fishing in that area. Sport fishing on streams or lakes on, or adjacent to, refuge units would be anticipated to be bank or boat fishing with moderate user numbers. Also, because most of the aquatic habitats on the refuge are limited to the Neches River and small lakes and streams, fishing tournaments will not be possible on the refuge.

Availability of Resources: Most of the refuge's units will be in remote rural, bottomland hardwood forested areas. At this time most parking facilities are limited to a few automobiles or all-terrain vehicles on dirt trails. There are a few existing public fishing access points at the intersection of major highways and the River. The refuge currently is managed as a satellite of the Little River National Wildlife Refuge Complex in Broken Bow, Oklahoma. Neches River National Wildlife Refuge's staff will consist of a manager who is stationed at Caddo Lake National Wildlife Refuge and will be assisted by personnel from the Little River National Wildlife Refuge for biological, clerical, law enforcement, and maintenance support.

Anticipated Impacts of the Use: If there is any question that a public use may harm Service trust species, the refuge manager should always decide for wildlife protection over public use. Recreational fishing occurring on migratory bird habitats may have only temporary or negligible effects on Service trust resources.

Public Review and Comment: This compatibility determination will be circulated for public review and comment with the Conceptual Management Plan, the Environmental Assessment, and Land Protection Plan for the proposed refuge for 45 days in 2005. The National Wildlife Refuge System Improvement Act of 1997 ensures wildlife photography, one of the six priority wildlife-dependent recreational uses, is considered for integration into refuge programs provided it is determined compatible with the purposes for which the refuge was established. The Act insures that lands added to the refuge System with existing compatible wildlife-dependent recreational uses will continue, pending completion of a comprehensive conservation plan for the refuge. With appropriate management, future use for wildlife photography should not affect accomplishment of the refuge purposes. The Act insures that the public is given an opportunity to participate in the process that determines whether or not an activity is compatible.

Determination (check one below):
____ **Use is not compatible**
_X_ **Use is Compatible with Following Stipulations**
Stipulations Necessary to Ensure Compatibility:
All state and federal fishing laws and license requirements will be followed.

Federal and /or State law enforcement agencies will ensure legal compliance, safety, and protection of refuge resources. Adequate staffing and funding or assistance from other agencies must be available to ensure a safe and quality fishing experience.

Public or legal access to tracts must be available. Access to the body waters must be safe.

Vehicle and/or all-terrain vehicle use may be restricted to prevent damage to refuge resources.

The refuge Manager must determine whether each proposed fishing program on the refuge will not materially interfere with or detract from the purpose for which the refuge was established.

Some areas may be subject to seasonal closure during migratory bird use periods.

Justification: The Service believes one of the key needs of our society is wildlife photography leading to an appreciation and advocacy of our natural resources. This is also a key goal for the Neches River National Wildlife Refuge as well.

Signatures: **Refuge Manager:**

_____
(Signature and Date)

Concurrence: Regional Chief:

_____
(Signature and Date)

Mandatory 10- or 15-year Re-evaluation Date:
_____2015_____

DRAFT INTERIM COMPATIBILITY DETERMINATION

Use: Recreational Fishing

Refuge Name: Neches River National Wildlife Refuge

Establishing and Acquisition Authorities: The Migratory Bird Conservation Act of 1929, as, amended, the Fish and Wildlife Act of 1956 and the Land and Water Conservation Fund Act of 1963, as amended.

Refuge Purposes: The purposes for the refuge will be:

- ... For the development, advancement, management, conservation, and protection of fish and wildlife resources ... 16 U.S.C. 742(b) (1)(Fish and Wildlife Act of 1956).
- ... For use as an inviolate sanctuary, or for any other management purpose, for migratory birds. 16 U.S.C. 715d (Migratory Bird Conservation Act)
- ... For the conservation of...wetlands...and to help fulfill international obligations contained in various migratory bird treaties and conventions. 16 U.S.C. 3901(b)

The refuge will be established to achieve the above listed purposes by:

- Protecting, restoring, and maintaining the bottomland hardwood forest plant community,

- Protecting and enhancing habitat for migratory bird use, and

- Protecting and enhancing habitats to sustain healthy populations of native fish and wildlife species.

This will be accomplished through an ecosystem approach that protects the bottomland hardwood plant community and wildlife resources.

National Wildlife Refuge System Mission: To administer a national network of lands and waters for the conservation, management, and where appropriate, restoration of the fish, wildlife, and plant resources and their habitats within the United States for the benefit of present and future generations of Americans.

Description of Use: Recreational Fishing

If areas are acquired that provide fishing opportunities and do not conflict with refuge management objectives, the Service will make every effort to provide fishing in that area. Sport fishing on streams or lakes on, or adjacent to, refuge units would be anticipated to be bank or boat fishing with moderate user numbers. Also, because most of the aquatic habitats on the refuge are limited to Neches River and small lakes and streams, fishing tournaments will not be possible on the refuge.

Availability of Resources: Most of the refuge's units will be in remote rural, bottomland hardwood forested areas. At this time most parking facilities are limited to a few automobiles on dirt trails. The refuge currently is managed as a satellite of the Little River National Wildlife Refuge Complex in Broken Bow, Oklahoma. Neches River National Wildlife Refuge's staff will consist of a manager who is stationed at Caddo Lake National Wildlife Refuge and will be assisted by personnel from the Little River National Wildlife Refuge for biological, clerical, law enforcement, and maintenance support.

Anticipated Impacts of the Use: If there is any question that a public use may harm Service trust species, the refuge manager should always decide for wildlife protection over public use. Recreational fishing occurring on migratory bird habitats may have only temporary or negligible effects on Service trust lands.

Public Review and Comment: This compatibility determination will be circulated for public review and comment with the Draft Conceptual Management Plan, the Environmental Assessment, and Land Protection Plan for the proposed refuge establishment for 45 days in 2005. The National Wildlife Refuge System Improvement Act of 1997 ensures wildlife photography, one of the six priority wildlife-dependent recreational uses, is considered for integration into refuge programs provided it is determined compatible with the purposes for which the refuge was established. The Act insures that lands added to the refuge System with existing compatible wildlife-dependent recreational uses will continue, pending completion of a comprehensive conservation plan for the refuge. With appropriate management, future use for wildlife photography should not affect accomplishment of the refuge purposes. The Act insures that the public is given an opportunity to participate in the process that determines whether or not an activity is compatible.

Determination (check one below):

_____ Use is not compatible

_X_ Use is Compatible with Following Stipulations

Stipulations Necessary to Ensure Compatibility:

All state and federal fishing laws and license requirements will be followed.

Federal and /or State law enforcement agencies will ensure legal compliance, safety, and protection of refuge resources. Adequate staffing and funding or assistance from other agencies must be available to ensure a safe and quality fishing experience.

Public or legal access to tracts must be available. Access to the body waters must be safe.

Vehicle and/or all-terrain vehicle use may be restricted to prevent damage to refuge resources.

The refuge Manager must determine whether each proposed fishing program on the refuge will not materially interfere with or detract from the purpose for which the refuge was established.

Some areas may be subject to seasonal closure during migratory bird use periods.

Justification: The Service believes one of the key needs of our society is wildlife photography leading to an appreciation and advocacy of our natural resources. This is also a key goal for the Neches River National Wildlife Refuge as well.

Signatures: **Refuge Manager:** _____

(Signature and Date)

Concurrence: Regional Chief: _____

(Signature and Date)

Mandatory 10- or 15-year Re-evaluation Date: _____2015_____

DRAFT INTERIM COMPATIBILITY DETERMINATION

Use: Environmental Education

Refuge Name: Neches River National Wildlife Refuge

Establishing and Acquisition Authorities: The Migratory Bird Conservation Act of 1929, as, amended, and the Fish and Wildlife Act of 1956 and the Land and Water Conservation Fund Act of 1963, as amended.

Refuge Purposes: The purposes for the refuge will be:

- ... For the development, advancement, management, conservation, and protection of fish and wildlife resources ...16 U.S.C. 742(b)(1)(Fish and Wildlife Act of 1956).
- ... For use as an inviolate sanctuary, or for any other management purpose, for migratory birds. 16 U.S.C. 715d (Migratory Bird Conservation Act)
- .. For the conservation of...wetlands...and to help fulfill international obligations contained in various migratory bird treaties and conventions. ÉÓ 16 U.S.C. ○ 3901(b)

The refuge will be established to achieve the above stated purposes by:

- Protecting, restoring, and maintaining the bottomland hardwood forest plant community,
- Protecting and enhancing habitat for migratory bird use, and
- Protecting and enhancing habitat to sustain healthy populations of native fish and wildlife species.

This will be accomplished through an ecosystem approach that protects the bottomland hardwood plant community and wildlife resources.

National Wildlife Refuge System Mission: To administer a national network of lands and waters for the conservation, management, and where appropriate, restoration of the fish, wildlife, and plant resources and their habitats within the United States for the benefit of present and future generations of Americans.

Description of Use: Environmental Education

This use typically involves groups of students of varying ages observing on-site presentations by teachers or guides about the biological or ecological topics regarding the site.

Availability of Resources: Most of the refuge's units will be in remote rural, bottomland hardwood forested areas. At this time most parking facilities are limited to a few automobiles on dirt trails. The refuge currently is managed as a satellite of the Little River National Wildlife Refuge Complex in Broken Bow, Oklahoma. Neches River National Wildlife Refuge's staff will consists of a manager who is stationed at Caddo Lake National Wildlife Refuge and will be assisted by personnel from the Little River National Wildlife Refuge for biological, clerical, law enforcement, and maintenance support.

Anticipated Impacts of the Use: If there is any question that a public use may harm Service trust species, the refuge manager should always decide for wildlife protection over public use. Environmental education practiced on migratory bird habitats may have only temporary or negligible effects on Service trust resources.

Public Review and Comment: This compatibility determination will be circulated for public review and comment with the Draft Conceptual Management Plan, the Environmental Assessment, and Land Protection Plan for the proposed refuge establishment for 45 days in 2005. The National Wildlife Refuge System Improvement Act of 1997 ensures wildlife photography, one of the six priority wildlife-dependent recreational uses, is considered for integration into refuge programs provided it is determined compatible with the purposes for which the refuge was established. The Act insures that lands added to the refuge System with existing compatible wildlife-dependent recreational uses will continue, pending completion of a comprehensive conservation plan for the refuge. With appropriate management, future use for wildlife photography should not affect accomplishment of the refuge purposes. The Act insures that the public is given an opportunity to participate in the process that determines whether or not an activity is compatible.

Determination (check one below):

_____ Use is not compatible

_X_ Use is Compatible with Following Stipulations

Stipulations Necessary to Ensure Compatibility:

Public or legal access to tracts must be available.

Vehicle and/or all-terrain vehicle use may be restricted to prevent damage to refuge resources.

Some areas may be subject to seasonal closures during migratory bird use periods.

Justification: The Service believes one of the key needs of our society is environmental education leading to an appreciation and advocacy of our natural resources. This is also a key goal for the Neches River National Wildlife Refuge as well.

Signatures: **Refuge Manager:** _____

(Signature and Date)

Concurrence: Regional Chief: _____

(Signature and Date)

Mandatory 10- or 15-year Re-evaluation Date: _____2015_____

DRAFT INTERIM COMPATIBILITY DETERMINATION

Use: Hunting

Refuge Name: Neches River National Wildlife Refuge

Establishing and Acquisition Authorities: The Migratory Bird Conservation Act of 1929, as, amended, the Fish and Wildlife Act of 1956 and the Land and Water Conservation Fund Act of 1963, as amended.

Refuge Purposes: The purposes for the refuge will be:

- .. For the development, advancement, management, conservation, and protection of fish and wildlife resources ...16 U.S.C. 742(b)(1)(Fish and Wildlife Act of 1956).
- .. For use as an inviolate sanctuary, or for any other management purpose, for migratory birds. 16 U.S.C. 715d (Migratory Bird Conservation Act)
- .. For the conservation of...wetlands...and to help fulfill international obligations contained in various migratory bird treaties and conventions. 16 U.S.C. 3901(b)

The refuge will be established to achieve the above referenced purposes by:

- Protecting, restoring, and maintaining the bottomland hardwood forest plant community,
- Protecting and enhancing habitat for migratory bird use, and
- Protecting and enhancing habitats to sustain healthy populations of native fish and wildlife species.

This will be accomplished through an ecosystem approach that protects the bottomland hardwood plant community and wildlife resources.

National Wildlife Refuge System Mission: To administer a national network of lands and waters for the conservation, management, and where appropriate, restoration of the fish, wildlife, and plant resources and their habitats within the United States for the benefit of present and future generations of Americans.

Description of Use: Hunting

Recreational objectives do provide opportunities for limited hunting. Deer, turkey, squirrel, rabbit, raccoon and waterfowl hunting could be possible on the refuge. Deer hunting may be archery, muzzle loader, shot gun or rifle hunting. Raccoon hunting will be limited to walk in only.

Availability of Resources: Most of the refuge's units will be in remote rural, bottomland hardwood forested areas. At this time most parking facilities are limited to a few automobiles on dirt trails. The refuge currently is managed as a satellite of the Little River National Wildlife Refuge Complex in Broken Bow, Oklahoma. Neches River National Wildlife Refuge's staff will consist of a manager who is stationed at Caddo Lake National Wildlife Refuge and will be assisted by personnel from the Little River National Wildlife Refuge for biological, clerical, law enforcement, and maintenance support.

Anticipated Impacts of the Use: If there is any question that a public use may harm Service trust species, the refuge manager should always decide for wildlife protection over public use. Hunting practiced on migratory bird habitats may have only temporary or negligible effects on Service trust resources.

Public Review and Comment: This compatibility determination will be circulated for public review and comment with the Conceptual Management Plan, the Environmental Assessment, and Land Protection Plan for the proposed refuge establishment for 45 days in 2005. The National Wildlife Refuge System Improvement Act of 1997 ensures wildlife photography, one of the six priority wildlife-dependent recreational uses, is considered for integration into refuge programs provided it is determined compatible with the purposes for which the refuge was established. The Act insures that lands added to the refuge System with existing compatible wildlife-dependent recreational uses will continue, pending completion of a comprehensive conservation plan for the refuge. With appropriate management, future use for wildlife photography should not affect accomplishment of the refuge purposes. The Act insures that the public is given an opportunity to participate in the process that determines whether or not an activity is compatible.

Determination (check one below):

____ **Use is not compatible**

_X_ **Use is Compatible with Following Stipulations**

Stipulations Necessary to Ensure Compatibility:

All state and federal hunting laws and license requirements will be followed.

Federal and/or State law enforcement agencies will ensure legal compliance, safety, and protection of refuge resources. Adequate staffing and funding or assistance from other agencies must be available to ensure a safe and quality hunting experience.

Public or legal access to tracts must be available. Refuge units must be sufficient in size to accommodate safe and quality hunting experiences without endangering neighboring private properties.

More allowances for unit size and availability may be made for archery hunting over firearm hunting, i.e., smaller units may be able to accommodate archery hunting, but not firearm hunting. Vehicle and/or all-terrain vehicle use may be restricted to prevent damage to refuge resources. Many of the refuge roads will be on wet terrain and may be vulnerable to erosion/siltation exacerbated by frequent vehicle use.

The refuge manager must determine whether each proposed hunting program on the refuge will not materially interfere with or detract from the purpose for which the refuge was established.

The refuge manager must determine an appropriate daily hunter capacity limit for each unit where hunting will take place, so that hunter experiences are safe and high quality and that resources will not be impaired. The refuge manager must implement appropriate hunter capacity control measures as needed.

Some areas may be subject to seasonal closure during migratory bird use periods.

Justification: The Service believes one of the key needs of our society is hunting leading to an appreciation and advocacy of our natural resources. This is also a key goal for the Neches River National Wildlife Refuge as well.

Signatures: **Refuge Manager:**

_____

(Signature and Date)

Concurrence: Regional Chief:

_____

(Signature and Date)

Mandatory 10- or 15-year Re-evaluation Date:
      _____2015_____

Appendix 6: Endangered Species Act Section 7 Consultation

INTRA-SERVICE SECTION 7 BIOLOGICAL EVALUATION FORM

Originating Person: JeannieWagner-Greven____
Telephone Number: __505-248-6633_____
Date: _September 10, 2004_____

2-12-05-I-010

I.   **Region: 2**

II.   **Service Activity (Program): Planning Division, Proposed Neches River National Wildlife Refuge**

III.   **Pertinent Species and Habitat:** (These were taken from the county lists on our Intranet site).

    A.   Listed species and/or their critical habitat within the action area:
red-cockaded woodpecker, bald eagle, Louisiana black bear It is not known if any species are actually found in the project area.
A colony of red-cockaded woodpeckers has been documented east and adjacent to the project area in the I.D. Fairchild State Forest. This is in the historic range for Louisiana black bears. Some local biologists believe Louisiana black bears are reintroducing themselves into suitable available habitat in their former East Texas range, and are slowly expanding westward, but it is unlikely that they have reached the project area at this time.

    B.   Proposed species and/or proposed critical habitat within the action area: None

    C.   Candidate species within the action area: Louisiana pine snake, Neches River rose-mallow It is not known if any species are actually found in the project area.

    D.   Include species/habitat occurrence on a map:

IV.   **Geographic area or station name and action: Proposed Neches River National Wildlife Refuge, Anderson and Cherokee Counties, Texas**

V.   **Location (attach map):**

    A.   Ecoregion Number and Name: **East Texas**

    B.   County and state: **Anderson and Cherokee Counties, Texas**

    C.   Section, township, and range (or latitude and longitude): **Latitude: 31 degrees, 47 minutes North; Longitude: 95 degrees, 20 minutes West**

    D.   Distance (miles) and direction to nearest town: **Approximately 15 miles northeast to Jacksonville**

E. Species/habitat occurrence: It is not known if any species are actually found in the project area.

VI. **Description of proposed action (attach additional pages as needed): Proposed establishment of the Neches River National Wildlife Refuge**

VII. **Determination of Effects:**

A. Explanation of effects of the action on species and critical habitat in items III A, B, and C (attach additional pages as needed): **Protecting habitat will have no adverse effects on any known listed species. Possible future management activities will be evaluated first for effects on species of concern and would be rejected or modified if there were potential adverse effects.**

B. Explanation of actions to be implemented to reduce adverse effects:

VIII. **Effect determination and response requested:**   [* = optional]

A. Listed species/designated critical habitat:

Determination   Response Requested

No effect on species/critical habitat
(species:_red-cockaded woodpecker, bald eagle,
Louisiana black bear_____)   __**X**___ *Concurrence

May affect, is not likely to adversely affect species
/critical habitat
(species: _____Concurrence

May affect, is likely to adversely affect species
/critical habitat
(species:_____)   _____Formal Consultation

B. Proposed species/proposed critical habitat:

Determination   Response Requested

No effect on proposed species/critical habitat
(species:_____)   ___**X**__ *Concurrence

Is not likely to jeopardize proposed species/
adversely modify proposed critical habitat
(species:_____)   _____ Concurrence

Is likely to jeopardize proposed species/
  adversely modify proposed critical habitat
(species:_____)   _____ Conference

C.   Candidate species:

<u>Determination</u>   <u>Response Requested</u>

No effect on candidate species
(species: Louisiana pine snake, Neches
 River rose-mallow_)   ___**X**__*Concurrence

Is not likely to jeopardize candidate species
(species:_____)   _____ Concurrence

Is likely to jeopardize candidate species
(species:_____)   _____ Conference

D. Remarks (attach additional pages as needed): **Contact Jim Neal 936-569-6129 or Jeffrey Reid 936-639-8546 for additional technical information.** Two rare plant species, Texas spice tree and <u>Geocarpum minimum</u>, are documented on the project area.

_____   9-16-04
Signature and Title   **Date**
[Title/office of supervisor at originating office]

IX.   **Reviewing ESFO Evaluations:**

A.   Concurrence: ___✓___   Nonconcurrence: _____

B.   Formal consultation required: _____

C.   Conference required _____

D.   Informal conference required _____

E.   Remarks (attach additional pages as needed):

_____   10/14/04
Signature and Title   **Date**
[Title/office of reviewing official]

Appendix 7: List of Preparers

Jeannie Wagner-Greven, Assistant Refuge Supervisor, R2
Thomas P. Baca, Chief, Division of Planning, NWRS, R2
Mark Williams, Refuge Manager, Caddo Lake NWR, Texas
Kari McGuire, Planning Intern, Division of Planning
Jim Neal, Wildlife Biologist, Division of Migratory Birds
Yvette Truitt, Wildlife Biologist, Division of Planning
Doug St. Pierre, Senior Planner, Division of Planning
Kelly Thompson, Office Assistant, Division of Planning